Holy Cross Chu...

RAMSBURY

Holy Cross Church

RAMSBURY

A guide, history and meditation

Barbara Croucher

*'You made us for Yourself, and our hearts are restless
until they rest in You.'*

Augustine of Hippo (AD 354 – 430)

B

First published 2005 by Barbara Croucher
25 Ashley Piece, Ramsbury
Marlborough, Wiltshire SN8 2QE.

ISBN 0-9511293-2-5

This book is printed on paper made from fully managed and sustained forest sources.

Printed in England by Alden Group Limited, Oxford.

A catalogue record for this book is available from the British Library.

Design by Simon Orton, Orton Design Limited,
5 Old Theatre Place, Ramsbury, Wiltshire SN8 2QS.

Front cover photo by David Stevens.

Back cover photo by Duncan Croucher.

CONTENTS

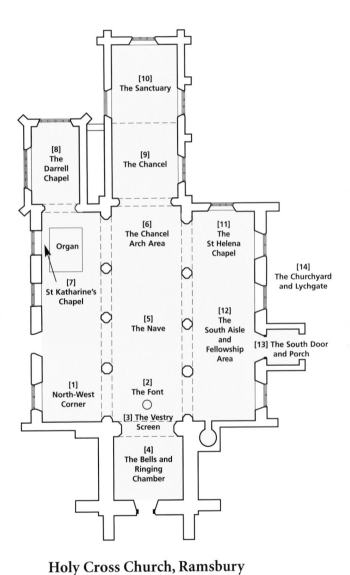

Holy Cross Church, Ramsbury

ABOUT THIS BOOK

Thank you to those people, both locals and visitors, who asked for more of a guide to Holy Cross than the small leaflet currently available, thus instilling the idea of this book into my mind.

Thank you to friends for their encouragement: to Mike Stokes for getting me started, as the blank paper stared up at me, to Jane Handford for her valuable comments on an early draft, to the Revd John Railton, our Rector, for his most helpful suggestions and Foreword, and to Bishop Peter Hullah for his thoughts and reflections in the Preface. I am also grateful to Jon Cannon, architectural historian, for his helpful comments on dating parts of the church.

I am indebted to Professor Rosemary Cramp of Durham University, the leading authority on Anglo-Saxon carving, for her very generous sharing of her research on our Anglo-Saxon stones. That section of the book is based almost entirely on her work, and I am very grateful to her.

It has been a privilege to have one of the UK's leading architectural photographers, David Stevens, of Downland Partnership, Ramsbury, to take photographs of the major features in Holy Cross. Yesterday St Paul's Cathedral, today Holy Cross, Ramsbury – thank you, David!

Photographs nowadays often need a tailor to stitch them together. I am grateful to my husband, Duncan, who has spent many hours stitching together on computer the stained glass and the Anglo-Saxon stones, as well as providing many other photographs. My thanks also to Julia Wilkins for the Lychgate photograph.

Eric Kilner has again generously responded to my request for sketches of particular features in the church using his wonderfully skilful pen, and I thank him for them. Also, a special thank you to Mary Gamester for her serpent drawing, and her support with architectural research.

Keeping this book very much created in Ramsbury, I am hugely grateful to Simon Orton for his inspired design work. Undertaken in a calm and gentle way, he rose to the challenge of combining the architecture, history and spirituality which I have tried to reflect.

Finally, thank you especially to Louise Palmer, and to David Jordon and Peter Rapson, for their great generosity.

Notes for the use of this guide:

No church can be fully explained without a detailed excavation: inside, outside and in the walls. This has not been done for Holy Cross, therefore this guide cannot be the definitive story.

- If you simply want a brief guided tour of the church, read the text in bold at the beginning of each section.
- If you would like to know more, this can be found in the rest of the text and at the end under 'Appendix 1: Further points of interest'.
- You may like to spend time with your own thoughts, in prayer or meditation. The Bible texts, prayers and poems are there for guidance if you wish to use them.

Profits from the sale of this guide will go towards the work of the Church in the community of Ramsbury.

DEDICATION
To the glory of God

Holy Cross is not simply a lovely Grade 1 listed building, but also a place where we may be touched by God, in prayer and stillness, worship and celebration, grief and joy. Writing this book has not been easy as I confront God and my faith, in the reality of a life-shortening, incurable disease. My hope is that something in this book and church will touch you. God never forces Himself on us, but He's always there, with us every moment, if only we pause to listen, to 'be'.

THE DIFFERENCE

*I got up early one morning and
rushed right into the day;
I had so much to accomplish that I
didn't have time to pray.
Problems just tumbled about me,
and heavier came each task.
'Why doesn't God help?' I wondered.
He answered, `You didn't ask.'*

*I wanted to see joy and beauty, but
the day toiled on, grey and bleak.
I wondered why God didn't show me.
He said 'But you didn't seek.'
I tried to come into God's presence;
I used all my keys at the lock;
God gently and lovingly chided,
'My child, you didn't knock.'*

*I woke up early this morning,
and paused before entering the day:
I had so much to accomplish
that I had to take time to pray.*

Florence Hood

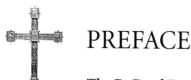

PREFACE

The Rt Revd Peter Hullah, *13th Bishop of Ramsbury*

Show me your ways, O Lord, and teach me your paths.

Psalm 25:4

Welcome to Holy Cross Church, Ramsbury and thank you, Barbara Croucher, for writing this guide with such precision and care. Thank you for sharing with us, in a very special way, your love of local history and your faith.

For over a thousand years this church has been a holy place on sacred ground where men and women have met God, worshipped God and learnt of God's ways.

In this lovely church, set at the heart of the community, we learn how each generation has created and built in reponse to God's call.

As we visit Holy Cross, we find living history, stones, designs and pictures which tell stories of the way God acts in the life and death of the risen life of Jesus.

This guide helps us learn more about how this community has changed and grown over the centuries, how faith has come alive and how life and death, sorrows and joys have been brought here to be treasured and remembered.

In learning more about the features of this church we discover how personal and community life are patterned and moulded through baptism, by the Eucharist, in marriage and in death, for service locally and for the world. As you visit, look for signs today of our local church life within the Whitton team in the Diocese of Salisbury and ecumenically. Look for signs of our links, in service and in prayer, with the Episcopal Church in the Sudan.

As we walk around the church, this guide becomes a living guide for our spiritual journey. The readings and commentary invite us to pause and to reflect, to meditate and to pray. Through following a path here in church we may discover more of God's way for us and how we can respond to God's call to us.

I hope that you will enjoy and be inspired by your visit to Holy Cross Church, Ramsbury.

May the peace of this church enable you to learn more of the history of this community.
May the spirit of God inspire you to enter into God's presence.
May the light of Christ be a lamp to guide you along the way and may you, and those
whom you love, find God's blessing here.

+ Peter Ramsbury

Holy Cross Church, Ramsbury by Buckler, c.1806

Places permeated by years of prayer are 'thin' places,

where we can become conscious of the interweaving of the timelessness

and love of God with our own reality.

FOREWORD

The Revd Dr John Railton, *Rector, Whitton Benefice*

Barbara Croucher is well-known as a local researcher and historian, and author of a number of books about the community in and around this lovely old village of Ramsbury. The Parish Church of Holy Cross is an important part of the community and a focus for many aspects of community as well as spiritual life. Not even the most casual day visitor could fail to be touched and moved by the sense of the eternal in the atmosphere of this ancient building, and those who worship here regularly are always conscious of the privilege of gathering and praying in a place where God has been worshipped continuously 'since time immemorial'.

   In this book, Barbara brings together a deep appreciation of the history and archaeology of the church building and the community which it serves, but especially of the way in which its story has evolved through the lives and experience of the people who have lived here and contributed to the life and development of the community, and offers it as a channel for growing understanding. As she leads her readers on a journey round the church building and invites them to reflect and pray on key aspects of faith, so God invites them to move forward on their own personal journeys of faith and into a deeper relationship with Him, the very source of all being.

I warmly commend this book which I know you will enjoy.

John Railton

WELCOME to the church of the Holy Cross, Ramsbury

This building, probably raised on the site of an Anglo-Saxon cathedral, has been a place where people have come to pray, and to worship God, since it was built in the thirteenth century. Over a thousand years of prayer in one place instills a quality to the silence. You may like to pause for a moment and breathe in the stillness.

Churches are built to be houses of God; their spiritual power can take us beyond ourselves, challenge us, raise questions about the meaning and purpose of life, what it is for and how we are to use it.

Holy places call us out of the stress, chaos and conflict of daily living, and allow us to breathe in the peace – relax – let go – and in the stillness 'know that I am God.'

'Be still and know that I am God.'

Psalm 46:10

INTRODUCTION

Although the first evidence of settlement so far discovered at Ramsbury, after the Romans left the valley, is of a seventh or eighth century iron-smelting forge site in the High Street, the earliest evidence of Christianity lies in the Anglo-Saxon stones, set out now in the north-west corner of the church. The date of the stones, which include parts of two crosses, is uncertain but thought to be about AD 860 or into the next century.

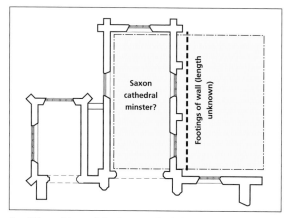

Possible positions of the Saxon cathedral minster, relating to the footings of a wall discovered in 1891.

From 909 to 1058 a bishopric was established at Ramsbury, and it was thought a cathedral minster church was built somewhere on the site of the present church. Although nothing can be seen of this Anglo-Saxon cathedral, some footings of a wall, running parallel to but three feet to the south of the chancel, were discovered in 1891.

However, the present building dates from the thirteenth century, when the chancel and first part of the nave, possibly with narrow aisles, were built. The nave was extended, two transept side chapels added, and the tower built, in the early fourteenth century.

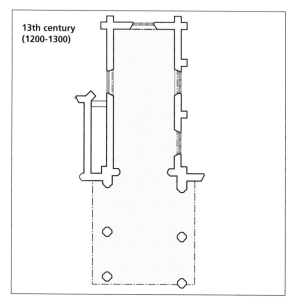

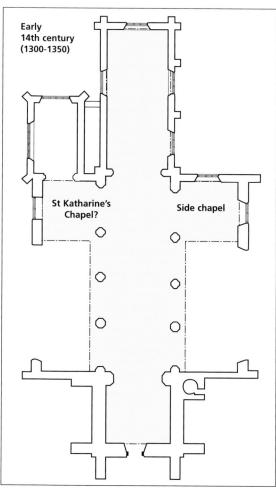

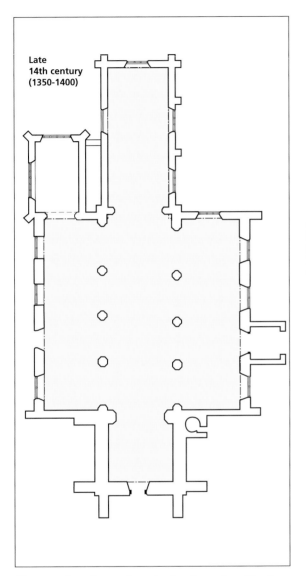

Late
14th century
(1350-1400)

church. This made the nave much darker so in the sixteenth century the nave walls were raised and clerestory windows inserted for more light. At the same time the lower pitch roof was constructed.

The Darrell Chapel was an early fifteenth century addition, built by the Calston family of Littlecote, which passed by marriage to the Darrells.

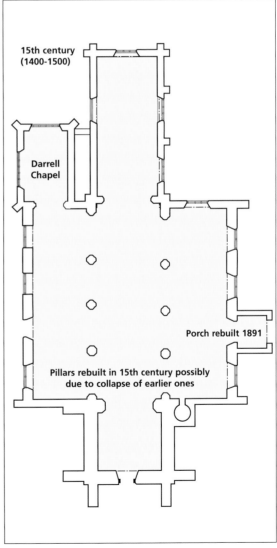

15th century
(1400-1500)

Darrell
Chapel

Porch rebuilt 1891

Pillars rebuilt in 15th century possibly
due to collapse of earlier ones

The remains of an arch springing from the pillar by the organ may have been part of the north transept.

Notice the different styles of moulding of the back pillars compared to the front ones. It is possible the back of the nave was rebuilt for some reason in the late fourteenth or early fifteenth centuries.

Later in the fourteenth century the transepts were extended westwards to form north and south aisles, creating the present square shape of the

The church was built for the Roman Catholic faith, which had become dominant at the Synod of Whitby in AD 664, pushing Celtic Christianity to the fringes of the British Isles. The change from the Roman Catholic to Protestant liturgy during the Reformation from 1533-58 brought turmoil and upheaval to the community. The wall paintings, rood screen, icons, statues and other decoration associated with Roman Catholicism would probably have been removed or destroyed at this time.

Some damage was done to the church during the Civil War (1642-51), and it is thought this was when the brasses were stripped from tombs in the chancel and Darrell chapel.

A choir and singers gallery across the west end was built in 1698-9, and side aisle galleries in 1788 when the roofs of both these aisles were first remade.

Repairs through the centuries were not enough to prevent the structure becoming unsafe so that in 1891 a major restoration, at a cost of £6000 (now £372,000) was undertaken. This, while removing much of historical interest, such as the box pews and singers' gallery, saved the church for use by future generations.

Site: Holy Cross church stands on an 'island' in the middle of the village. This 'island' may have been the extent of the original Anglo-Saxon 'burgh'. A pre-Christian cemetery may have existed on the site of the present graveyard. The first Anglo-Saxon churches were built around AD 650, usually on land already cleared and settled, with Anglo-Saxon minsters tending to be built on 'island' sites, providing further evidence that the original Anglo-Saxon church at Ramsbury may have been a minster. It was the focal point for all community activity and the church was the dominant building in the village.

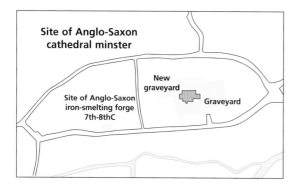

Although the north and south aisles were rebuilt in 1891, the original stone dressings were put back in their late-fourteenth century positions, so the church is essentially in the same form as when it was built. The present roofs of the side aisles were again remade then.

The south porch was also constructed at this time, replacing a smaller, less ornate one.

Minster: (administer) a district church, attached to a religious community, which acted as a missionary centre where priests lived communally, going out to convert and minister to the surrounding population. There were few priests at Ramsbury; just a small group were recorded in the 1086 Domesday Survey.

The spread of Christianity to Ramsbury:

The conversion of the Roman Emperor Constantine in AD 310 led to the spread of Christianity throughout the Roman Empire. Possibly the Orpheus temple *(below)* at the Littlecote Roman villa two miles from Ramsbury, saw Christian worship.

Between AD 449-600, the heathen Saxon Germanic peoples invaded the country, pushing Christianity to the Celtic fringes. Then St Columba crossed from Ireland to Iona in AD 563 and from Rome, Pope Gregory sent Augustine to Britain with 40 monks of his Benedictine order. From a base in Canterbury, the Christian faith spread rapidly through Anglo-Saxon Britain. We don't know when Ramsbury's Anglo-Saxon minster was built but by AD 909 a bishopric had been established here. It is suggested that the minster might have been a large and architecturally elaborate building.

Holy Cross: This was one of the earliest dedications for churches and might have been taken from the original Anglo-Saxon cathedral minster. The Holy Cross feast days of the Invention and Exaltation of the Cross fall on 3 May and 14 September respectively. In 1240, the King granted to the Bishop of Salisbury the right to hold a fair annually at Ramsbury on each date. Every year 14 September is still celebrated in Holy Cross.

'O Gracious and Holy Father, give us wisdom to perceive You, intelligence to understand You, diligence to seek You, eyes to behold You, and a heart to meditate on You, through the power of the Spirit of Jesus Christ, our Lord.'

St Benedict (480-543), founder of the Benedictine monastic movement.

Walk to the far side of the church and stand in front of the raised stone plinth. →

THE NORTH-WEST CORNER [1]

The Anglo-Saxon stones

The most significant historical objects in the church are the Anglo-Saxon stones. They were discovered during the 1891 restoration, in the south-east angle of the east wall of the nave or lying just below the ground against the foundations of that wall.

Carved in Bath stone, they mainly consist of: portions of three monumental slabs, the base stone of an upright cross, and two lengths of the shaft of another cross. The upright stones in front of you are from these two Anglo-Saxon crosses, which may have stood in the churchyard, providing a focus in the burial ground before the Anglo-Saxon cathedral minster was built.

This is an archaeologically important centre of Anglo-Saxon stone carving, dating from the ninth and tenth centuries. Notice the intricacy of the carving on the stones.

Descriptions of the stones

a) The cross (top stone of upright)
Probably of ninth century date, before the foundation of the see of Ramsbury.

EAST

Roundels enclosing crouched canine-like quadrupeds, with heads turned back, biting their own tails. Possibly inspired by European, Coptic or near Eastern art.

NORTH
These paired figure-of-eight motifs were common in Wessex and throughout Anglo-Saxon England. They were most popular after the end of the eighth century and were possibly inspired by Mediterranean carving.

WEST
Roundels of leonine creatures similar to the east face but with heads hanging down and the tails penetrating the back of the neck. No other sculptures have yet been found like these anywhere else.

Circle me Lord
Keep protection near and danger afar.
Circle me Lord
Keep hope within
Keep doubt without.
Circle me Lord
Keep light near
And darkness afar.
Circle me Lord
Keep peace within keep evil out.

David Adam

SOUTH
This interlaced motif is also a unique pattern in Anglo-Saxon sculpture.

b) Cross-shaft
The central stone is worn or re-dressed but the one face, with two reptilian creatures on it, are so similar to the base stone carving that it is very likely part of the same cross. It is also ninth or tenth century in date.

c) Base of cross-shaft

Probably ninth or tenth century.

EAST

Trace the complete body of a serpent-like beast, coiling from the tail at the base to its head at the top. The head, with two eyes, is biting its body. The body is decorated with chevron patterns and the beast is intertwined with interlace carving.

Serpents: Christianity used religious symbolism to teach those who couldn't read. An ancient serpent cult flourished in Ireland and Scotland long before the Celts came to Britain. When the Roman church customs replaced the Celtic at the Synod of Whitby in AD 664, the Celts encoded their traditions into sculpture, such as on crosses. The Vikings and Danes also had a serpent lore, representing blessing and rejuvenation.

In Genesis the serpent in the Garden of Eden was demonised, for Moses it was a healing icon, and Jesus spoke of its wisdom: 'be wise as serpents' (Matthew 10:16).

When shown in a spiral they are thought to represent the cycle of evolution and reincarnation. The circle created by biting itself was regarded as a symbol of eternity.

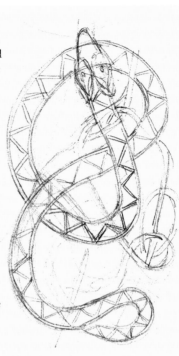

NORTH
Another complete serpent-like animal, coiling from a thin tail of interlace broadening to its head. This is in profile, biting its own body with sharp teeth. The body is again decorated with chevrons and tightly fettered with interlace patterns.

SOUTH
Further pairs of pattern C knots.

Professor Rosemary Cramp, the leading authority on Anglo-Saxon carving, writes: 'The composition is full of writhing life, and the savage biting at their own bodies, as well as the fetters and chains with which they are tightly bound, give these creatures a demonic appearance. If one is to see a religious significance in these panels then it must surely be as evil forces bound.' [1]

d) Part of domed grave cover

This grave cover, with its animal roundels, rosette patterns and figure-of-eight knots, suggest it is of the same date as the cross a) above. It may well have been the slab covering the grave, with the cross at its head, all possibly worked by the same person.

Notice the canine heads with their tongues joined together in an interlaced knot.

This type of grave cover was uncommon in Anglo-Saxon England, and probably dates from the ninth century.

WEST
Rows of knots, known in Saxon carving terms as pattern C, with small pattern E at the top.

The vine: *is one of the representations of Jesus, who said: 'I am the vine'. It is also used to represent the movement of the soul.*

'I am the vine, you are the branches. Those who abide in Me and I in them bear much fruit, because apart from Me you can do nothing.'

John 15:5

e) Domed grave cover

The carving is of a twisted plant scroll emanating from a single stem. Each scroll ends in a long triangular leaf, which may be of a vine.

The shape of the grave cover is identical to d) above and, again, was uncommon. It probably dates from the ninth century.

f) Flat, rectangular grave cover

Probably the most important piece of all these stones, this may have been a grave cover for one of the early Bishops of Ramsbury. Although very worn, it is possible to make out an Agnus Dei in the centre of the raised cross. The Lamb is shown in a crouching position with its head held up, surrounded by traces of a halo. It perches on a panel with scallops, representing rocky ground. Below is interlace pattern and below that a figure with upstretched arms or wings. Other creatures, including another serpent-like animal, flank the cross.

It is suggested this is the apocalyptic Lamb, possibly surrounded by the symbols of the evangelists – the lion (Mark), calf (Luke), eagle (John) and man (Matthew) - as described in the Book of Revelation 5:6, 12, 13.

Professor Rosemary Cramp: 'It is the only piece from the Ramsbury collection which reflects its importance as an Episcopal site, and an awareness of the theological and liturgical themes which are so fully expressed in the literature of later Anglo-Saxon England. Since the Lamb of the Apocalypse can be cross-referenced with the Eucharistic sacrifice, but also represents not

Christ alone but His Church, this would be suitable iconography on a grave cover for a bishop, or high-ranking ecclesiastic.'[2]

Other fragments of stone may also be of ninth or tenth century, one possibly of clothing or hair, the only carving linked to a human in these stones. An early thirteenth century monumental slab bearing a foliated cross *(right)* had been used in the fourteenth century as a window arch, having been cut into four pieces. Another piece of stone has Norman dog-tooth carving on it.

The various other pieces, including floor tiles and bricks, are of a later date. The floor tiles are of a similar age to the font and may have come from the Bishops' palace. They are encaustic tiles with a special glaze.

Agnus Dei: *the Lamb of God represents Jesus. When holding a banner it is a symbol of His Resurrection.*

As human beings, we all have some 'sin' within us, in whatever form it takes; no one is perfect, only Christ was perfect. It is that sin which sets us apart from God, separates us from Him, so that we lose the knowledge of His presence with us. Our lives become frenetic, anxious, often full of anger or fear. We fill our days with busyness to provide some sort of meaning, with little of that peace in us 'which passes all understanding.' (Philippians 4:7)

Jesus died so that, through Him, we can be cleansed from our sins, thus removing the barrier between us and God – and therein lies joy, freedom and peace.

The Jews have an ongoing ritual of sacrifice, including killing lambs, as an offering for sin, but the Christian belief is that Jesus' death was the one, final sacrifice for our sins. Thus, the Agnus Dei represents Jesus as the ultimate sacrificial lamb. His love for all mankind is so great He gave His life so that we can, in the end, never be separated from God.

'Then I saw between the throne and the four living creatures and among the elders a Lamb standing as if it had been slaughtered.'

'Worthy is the Lamb that was slaughtered to receive power and wealth and wisdom and might and honour and glory and blessing!'

'Then I heard every creature in heaven and on earth and under the earth and in the sea, and all that is in them, singing, "To the One seated on the throne and to the Lamb be blessing and honour and glory and might, for ever and ever!" '

Revelation 5:6, 12, 13.

You may like to think for a moment of God's great love for you.

'For God so loved the world that He gave His only Son, so that everyone who believes in Him may not perish but have eternal life.'

John 3:16

War memorials

The names of those from Ramsbury who died in the two world wars are recorded on two memorials and on the war memorial cross outside the church. Those of the USAF 437th Troop Carrier Group who died are also recorded here.

The 437th Troop Carrier Group of the USAF were stationed on Springs Hill, to the south of the village, from January 1944 to February 1945. It was from the airfield there that troops were flown in gliders for the 'D' Day landings in Normandy in June 1944.

One memorial was put up in 1978, while the memorial naming all those who died in the operation was consecrated in 1989.

'No one has greater love than this, to lay down one's life for one's friends.'
John 15: 13

Now turn to the lists of Bishops and Vicars on either side of the north door. →

The Bishops and Vicars of Ramsbury

The see of Ramsbury was created in AD 909 and continued through to 1058, when it was combined with that of Sherborne. It was transferred in 1075 to Old Sarum and then to Salisbury where the present cathedral was built.

Three of the Bishops of Ramsbury became Archbishops of Canterbury. The title of Bishop of Ramsbury was revived in 1974. The present Bishop, the thirteenth, is an Area Bishop of Salisbury Diocese.

Prebends of Ramsbury and Axford were set up by the mid-twelfth century, but ceased in 1545. A vicarage was ordained in 1294. The parish of Ramsbury–cum-Axford became part of the Whitton Team benefice in 1973.

History of the see of Ramsbury: In AD 705 the West Saxon see of Winchester was divided into two, the second being at Sherborne. By chance, the Bishops of both sees died in the same year, AD 909, leaving both of them vacant and allowing some readjustment. Three new sees were created: Ramsbury, which covered Wiltshire and Berkshire, Wells for Somerset, and Crediton for Devon and Cornwall. Winchester kept Hampshire and Surrey, and Sherborne covered Dorset.

The Bishops of Ramsbury also had a seat at Sonning and another possibly at Wilton. They were supported by revenues from five great manors: Potterne, Cannings, Ramsbury, Old Sarum and Sonning, worth in total 300 hides in the 1086 Domesday Survey.

At Ramsbury they had a notable church, an estate of 90 hides and were served by a small cathedral establishment. But in the 1050s Bishop Herman complained that there was no adequate community of clerks so in 1058 the see was combined with Sherborne, before moving in 1075 to Old Sarum, a manor belonging to the Hundred of Ramsbury which happened to be vacant at that time, and then to Salisbury.

The move also followed a Council at Windsor held by the Archbishop of Canterbury, Lanfranc, in 1072, ordering those Anglo-Saxon bishops situated in villages or remote rural areas to be moved to major towns.

'Ecclesia Corvinensis':

The Bishops of Ramsbury signed themselves 'ecclesia corvinensis' (the church of the raven). The name 'Ramsbury' possibly comes from the Old English name 'Hraefn' meaning 'raven', hence Hraefn's burgh or fortified town. Hraefn may have been the name of a local Anglo-Saxon leader who first settled on the site.

Raven: A bird of omen, possessing outstanding intelligence, particularly concerned with battlefield knowledge, skill and martial abilities. Ravens are not especially common around Ramsbury, but a few have currently been seen along the Kennet valley.

'Consider the ravens: they neither sow nor reap, they have neither storehouse nor barn, and yet God feeds them. Of how much more value are you than the birds!'

Luke 12:24

The Anglo-Saxon Bishops:

The first Bishop of Ramsbury, Athelstan *(below)*, was succeeded by a Dane, Odo, a reformist and champion of Benedictine monasticism. The third Bishop, Aelfric, also held land in Blewbury, in Berkshire. Bishop Osulf was Odo's nephew. He died in AD 970 and was buried at Wilton. Alfstan, an exemplary monk from Abingdon, was a simple man, of great obedience. Another monk from Abingdon, Wulfgar, succeeded to the see. He was followed by Sigeric, a Glastonbury monk, who is

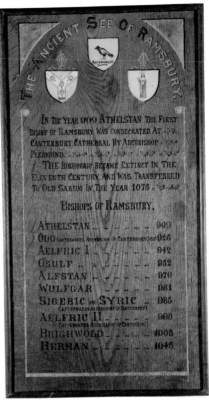

THE ANCIENT SEE OF RAMSBURY.

IN THE YEAR 909 ATHELSTAN THE FIRST BISHOP OF RAMSBURY WAS CONSECRATED AT CANTERBURY CATHEDRAL BY ARCHBISHOP PLEGMUND. THE BISHOPRIC BECAME EXTINCT IN THE ELEVENTH CENTURY AND WAS TRANSFERRED TO OLD SARUM IN THE YEAR 1075.

BISHOPS OF RAMSBURY.

ATHELSTAN	909
ODO (AFTERWARDS ARCHBISHOP OF CANTERBURY)	926
AELFRIC I	942
OSULF	952
ALFSTAN	970
WULFGAR	981
SIGEBIC or SYRIC (AFTERWARDS ARCHBISHOP OF CANTERBURY)	985
AELFRIC II (AFTERWARDS ARCHBISHOP OF CANTERBURY)	990
BRIGHWOLD	1005
HERMAN	1045

credited with the idea of paying Danegeld to prevent the Danes burning and pillaging the country.

Two more monks, Aelfric from Abingdon and Brighwold from Glastonbury, followed. Brighwold was a generous benefactor to his old monastery and may have passed money to it from Ramsbury, causing the bitter complaints from Herman, the tenth bishop, about the poverty of the see.

Odo and Sigeric became Archbishops of Canterbury and Aelfric II was nominated to the post but may not have been consecrated.

By 1086 the Domesday Survey records only a group of priests holding four hides as the remnants of the religious community.

The Bishops' Palace: A 'palace' for the Bishops of Ramsbury and then Salisbury, who took over as Lords of the Manor from 1075 to 1545, was built in the grounds of the present Ramsbury Manor, to the west of the village.

The house was crenellated in 1337 and 1377. It had a cloister, and a chapel where ordinations took place. Between 1520-21, Bishop Audley ordained three times in Salisbury cathedral, 48 times in Holy Cross church and 18 times in his chapel at the palace.

Prebends, rectors and vicars - origins of terms:

Prebend: the income of a canon or member of a chapter; the portion of
land or tithe from which this is drawn.

Prebendary: holder of a prebend; an honorary canon.

Rector: an incumbent of a Church of England parish where all the tithes
formerly passed to the incumbent.

Vicar: an incumbent of a Church of England parish where the tithes
formerly belonged to a chapter or religious house or to a layman.

Advowson: the right of presentation to a benefice or living; patronage.

Tithes: a tax of one tenth; a tenth part of the annual produce of land or
labour formerly levied to support the clergy and the church.

In 1086, Ramsbury church, with its remaining priests of the Anglo-Saxon
minster community, would have served the Hundred of Ramsbury. This
included the village and surrounds and also Bishopstone and Baydon. But
by 1091 it had passed to the canons of Salisbury, under the jurisdiction of
the Dean, as a Dean's Peculiar. It was named as part of the endowment in
the foundation charter for the cathedral there.

The cathedral chapter used the church's revenues to establish the prebends
of Ramsbury and Axford by the mid-twelfth century. The prebends were
replaced by the two prebends of Gillingham in 1545.

From the time a vicarage was ordained at Ramsbury, in 1294, to the end of
the prebendary in 1545, every known vicar was presented to the parish by a
prebendary. Thereafter, the advowson came either under the owner of the
Manor or the Crown. The last patron was Marjorie, Lady Burdett-Fisher,
step-daughter of Sir Francis Burdett, the last baronet, of Ramsbury Manor.

Income for the prebends and vicars came from the tithes, which were made compulsory in the tenth century at the
time the parish boundaries were delineated. The tithes were taken, first by the cathedral minster community at
Ramsbury, and when that ceased, by the prebendaries. Despite additional income from the prebendaries or the state,
the living of the vicar at Ramsbury remained poor.

Although the greater tithes of corn and hay normally went to the prebend or rector, in 1294 the vicar in Ramsbury
was given all corn tithes from the prebendary's demesne. In about 1323 some small tithes, such as milk, cheese and
vegetables, were added, either in kind, or as cash from the sale of calves, foals and lambs, and hay made in Axford. By
1756 the vicar, Richard Garrard, received two-thirds of his income from tithes, mostly cash, the remainder came from
fees and offerings. At the time of the enclosure of the common fields, in 1778, the vicar was given some land (glebe),
but in 1841 the tithe award commuted the tithes to rent.

In 1851 the vicar's annual income was made up from:

Land	£170
Tithe	£125
Glebe	£25
Other permanent endowment	£12
Fees	£18
Easter offerings	£6

Making a total of £356.

The vicar was also provided with a 'glebe' house, or vicarage.
The one in Ramsbury, just to the north of the church, was built in
1840, replacing an earlier vicarage on the same site. It was sold in
1967 when a new glebe house was built in Back Lane.

A story from the Rt Revd John Neale, 11th Bishop of Ramsbury:
'It was Paddington Station. I looked for a seat in a crowded train.
There was one left and I sat opposite a flush-faced gentleman who
had a military air. "My word," he said loudly, and turned to his
companion, "I do believe this man of the cloth is a Bishop!"
Then came the big question, "Pray, Sir, where is your see?" This
loud interrogation began to entertain the others. "I'm Bishop of
Ramsbury, in Wiltshire." My answer prompted the immediate
response, "How interesting, Bishop, I knew your predecessor."
Now was the time to hit the buffers. "Well" I said firmly, "that's
pretty strange; he died in 1078!" I hid behind my newspaper until
we reached home.'

Right: The Rt Revd John Neale, at the planting of the oak tree in the Square, 1986.
*Below right: The Rt Revd Peter Vaughan, 12th Bishop, with his wife, Elizabeth, on
the parish boundary walk, 1993.*
*Below: The Rt Revd Peter Hullah, with his wife Hilary, talking to the Prince of
Wales before the concert on 9 July 1999, organised by Music in Country Churches.*

The holy water stoup

**Holy water stoups are part of the Roman Catholic inheritance from
the early church. Water, which was blessed each Sunday, was put in a
bowl in the stoup so that as people entered and left the church they
could dip their fingers in the water and make a sign of the cross on**

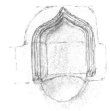

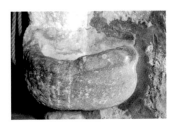

**their forehead or breast. This would remind
them of their baptismal vows, their need for cleansing from
sin, and the frailty of human life. Notice also the stoup to
the left of the south door. There is a third one on the centre
post at the foot of the steps to the tower (left), as this had
previously been accessed from the outside.**

*Now leave the area of the Saxon stones
and walk to the font.* →

THE FONT [2]

The bowl of the font is said to have been discovered in 1842 in the grounds of Ramsbury Manor, where the Bishops had formerly built a palace. Its date is not known but it may have been from the chapel of the medieval Bishops' palace. The base below the pedestal is of the same date as the bowl. The bowl is carved in a 'pineapple' design, which is very unusual. Inside are two fish and possibly two ichthyosaurus. Again, it is unusual to have the fish carved in the base of the bowl. The fish is one of the symbols of Jesus.

A local gentleman, Thomas Meyrick, had the pedestal carved to support the bowl. Representations of Jesus blessing the children, the passage of the Israelites through the Red Sea, Noah releasing the dove from the Ark, and Jonah cast up by the whale can be seen.

Before 1891, the font stood in what was the midwives corner where the Anglo-Saxon stones are now, and before that at the crossing.

Fish: Greek = *icthus. Icthus* also stands for the Greek *'Iesous Christos Theou Huios Soter* (Jesus Christ, Son of God, Saviour). Thus the fish is a symbol of Christ. It is shortened to *ihc* and appears around the church.

Fonts were usually placed at the west end of a church. When infant baptism was introduced in 1661 the large, tub-shaped bowls were placed on a stand. Thus the bowl is often earlier in date than the stand, as at Holy Cross.

Covers were not made before the thirteenth century. They were introduced by Henry III (1216-72) to stop people stealing the holy water. There are no markings on the rim of the bowl to suggest one was used on this font.

BAPTISM: *Baptism is one of the two Christian sacraments instituted by Jesus Himself. It marks the beginning of our journey of faith, which continues for the rest of our lives. The first step in response to God's love, it is central to our life and personal relationship with Christ, which brings a unique richness and fullness to life, even in the dark times.*

The water of baptism is a symbol of the cleansing power of God, through the gift of the Holy Spirit.

You may like to pause for a moment and reflect on your own journey of faith.

'And when Jesus had been baptised, just as He came up from the water, suddenly the heavens were opened to Him and He saw the Spirit of God descending like a dove and alighting on Him. And a voice from heaven said: "This is My Son, the Beloved, with whom I am well pleased". '

Matthew 3:16-17.

'Spirit of the living God fall afresh on me;
Spirit of the living God fall afresh on me.
Break me, melt me, mould me, fill me.
Spirit of the living God, fall afresh on me.'

Daniel Iverson

Now look at the vestry screen behind the font. →

THE VESTRY SCREEN [3]

Behind the font a vestry screen was completed in 1911 to commemorate the 1000th anniversary of the consecration of the first Bishop of Ramsbury, Athelstan, in AD 909. Carvings of Athelstan and the then Bishop of Salisbury, Bishop Wordsworth, are on the front of the screen.

The screen replaced the organ, which was moved in 1891 to its present position. The singers' gallery, spreading across the west end of the church, was also removed at this time.

The cross on top of the screen, with the angels on either side, indicates the dedication of the church to the Holy Cross.

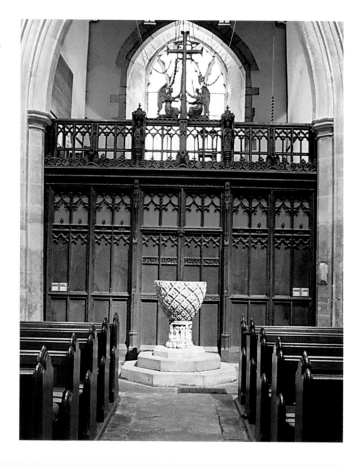

The plaque: 909-1909
'To the glory of God and in commemoration of the Thousandth Anniversary of the Consecration of Athelstan, first Bishop of Ramsbury, this screen was erected by public subscription and dedicated February 27th 1911. The completion of the work was made possible by the generosity of Ernest Salter Wills, Esquire, J.P. whilst tenant of Ramsbury Manor.'

The vestry was the original governing body of the parish, led by the churchwardens. Vestry meetings were either held in the church or at the Bell Inn, in the Square. It elected churchwardens, overseers of the poor, supervisors of the highways, and set the church rate, paid by every villager to cover parish and church expenses. This rate took over from the tithe (tenth)

payment begun in the tenth century.

After secular parish and rural district councils took over parish government from the vestry, churches continued to call the place they met for Parochial Church Council meetings, the vestry. Now it is used as a place for robing clergy and choirs, and for the needs of church services.

In the medieval period, the parish had to equip soldiers for home service so armour was kept in the church, probably in the vestry, in the safe keeping of the churchwardens. The Darrell Chapel, behind the organ, was formerly used as the vestry in Holy Cross when the parish bier and fire-fighting equipment were kept at the base of the tower. This area became the vestry when the responsibility for the fire brigade was transferred from the churchwardens to the new Parish Council in 1887.

The cross is central to the Christian faith as Jesus was put to death on a cross. The depiction of Jesus on the cross is called a crucifix *(below)*.

The cross was a spiritual symbol pre-dating Christianity but since Christ, various forms of the cross have been and still are used.

The Anglo-Saxon word for crucifix is rood. A crucifix always surmounted the rood screen in churches.

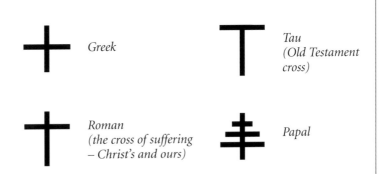

Greek

Tau (Old Testament cross)

Roman (the cross of suffering – Christ's and ours)

Papal

The cross and crucifix represent the agony and deep suffering Christ went through to break the power of death over us. In our times of suffering, pain and despair we can know that Jesus has been there too.

'My God, My God, why have You forsaken Me?'

Mark 15:34

'Because He Himself was tested by what He suffered, He is able to help those who are being tested.'

Hebrews 2:18

You may like to offer to God your own suffering, or that of others, and ask for His healing love to carry the burden, in whatever way that may be.

'Do not fear for I am with you, do not be afraid, for I am your God; I will strengthen you, I will help you, I will uphold you with my victorious right hand.'

Isaiah 41:10

17

Look above the vestry screen to the ringing chamber and tower. →

THE BELLS AND RINGING CHAMBER [4]

Above the vestry is the ringing chamber and bell tower, with a peel of six bells. Despite an active bell foundry at Aldbourne, two miles away, the bells were made by Abraham Rudhall, of Gloucester, in 1708, replacing a set of four bells and Sanctus, which were in the church in 1553. The tenor bell had to be re-cast in 1865. They are housed in a massive oak frame but the wide, solid tower gives an unusual amount of space for them.

Bell history: The earliest bells, apart from the Sanctus bell, were small ones which hung in the window apertures of the tower. From the twelfth century, bell foundries could cast larger bells but because of their weight, they needed strongly-built towers to support them, as at Holy Cross.

The ringing chamber, at a lower level, was accessed by an outside door on the south side of the tower before 1891. Then the outer door was blocked up, a new floor constructed and the internal door to the tower staircase used.

Inscriptions on the bells:

Treble: A : R 1708

Second: A : R 1708

Third: PEACE & GOOD
            NEIGHBOURHOOD
            A : R 1708

Fourth: ABRA: RVDHALL OF
            GLOUCESTER BELL
            FOUNDER 1708

Fifth: MR HAWES VICAR
            A : R 1708

Tenor: CAST BY JOHN WARNER
            & SONS LONDON 1865
            PATENT
            PROSPERITY TO THE CHURCH
            AND QUEEN. THIS BELL
            WAS RECAST
            AD 1865
            THE OLD BELL DATING BACK
            PRIOR TO 1553 BEING CRACKED.

This date of 1553 is incorrect as the new bell replaced the tenor cast in 1708 on which was inscribed:

Tenor: PROSPERITY TO THE CHURCH
            AND QUEEN. MATTHEW GILES
            THOMAS BEW EDWARD
            APPLEFORD CHURCHWARDENS
            A : R 1708

'Summoned by bells': Church bells were used to summon the villagers to church when they had no clocks in their homes. They were tolled for a curfew, at funerals, weddings, festivals, royal birthdays and military victories.

A Ramsbury notebook of 1903 records: 'The following rules are observed in the use of these bells. On Sundays the treble and second are chimed at 8 am and the tenor is raised and rung at 9 am. For the services all the bells are chimed for twenty-five minutes and the tenor is tolled for the last five minutes. At a death each bell is tolled (four strokes for a man and three strokes for a woman) all round, after which the tenor is raised and rung. At a funeral the fifth is tolled at minute intervals.

The bells are rung on the Greater Festivals.'

They are still rung regularly today, and on New Year's Eve, including the Millennium.

'In country churches old and pale
I hear the changes smoothly rung
And watch the coloured sallies fly
From rugged hands to rafters high
As round and back the bells are
swung.'

John Betjeman (1906-1984)
An Old-Marlburian who may have visited Ramsbury.
Reproduced by permission of John Murray Publishers.

As the bells call us to worship, so God calls us to Himself, to know Him intimately, to trust and rest in His love for each one of us:

'Thus says the Lord…who created you…who formed you:
Do not be afraid, for I have redeemed you;
I have called you by name, you are Mine.
When you pass through the waters,
I will be with you;
and through the rivers, they shall not overwhelm you;
When you walk through fire you shall not be burned, and the flame shall not consume you.
For I am the Lord your God,
the Holy One of Israel, your Saviour.'

Isaiah 43:1-3

Now turn from the vestry and font and look down the nave. →

THE NAVE [5]

Notice the fine, restored sixteenth-century roof with tie beams and carved heads on the bosses. The grotesque carvings may have been placed there for decoration and possibly also to protect the church from the dragons and demons thought to infest churches in medieval times. One of the bosses, to the right of the bell ringing chamber is of a fox. The angels, conspicuously and symbolically only at the eastern end of the nave, hold coats of arms, which may be those of donors to the new roof, or of instruments of the Passion.

Evidence of an earlier higher-pitched nave roof can be seen on the outside of the tower. The clerestory was built at the same time as the sixteenth-century lower-pitched roof.

The nave was the domain of the villagers and the walls were painted with biblical scenes to help them understand the Scriptures when few could read and before Bibles were generally available. Remnants of frescoes in 1891 were in such bad condition that, sadly, they were removed and the walls replastered.

The change in date between the thirteenth century front of the nave and fourteenth century back can be seen in the different styles of the pillars, although the back pillars are thought to be older than the tower, so they may have replaced earlier ones.

The pews were made from oak trees from Baydon, a few miles away. The wood grain indicates they had grown on chalk where growth is slower than on other soils. They replaced box pews which were removed in 1891.

Seating only appeared in churches when sermons increased in importance in the fifteenth century. Before that, the congregation stood or the sick and elderly sat on stone benches against the walls, hence the expression 'going to the wall'.

The two fine, brass chandeliers are dated 1751 and cost £22.16s.6d. The money was raised by subscription by the vicar, Richard Garrard, and churchwarden, Benjamin Symonds. Each is surmounted by a dove, a symbol of the Holy Spirit. It has been variously suggested that they were either of Dutch origin, or made by a Bristol firm which copied continental brasswork, or were from a workshop possibly at Oxford.

Roofs: Thirteenth-century church roofs were generally steep-pitched to throw off the rain and snow, and covered in thatch, tiles or even lead. When it was realised lead wouldn't slide or creep with expansion and contraction on a shallower-pitch roof, nave roofs were lowered. The old drip mould of the higher pitch can be seen on the east face of the tower.

The nave, aisles and tower have lead roofs, but the chancel is still covered in Westmoreland tiles.

The medieval church in the life of the villagers: The size of Holy Cross in the Middle Ages reflected the wealth of the Lords of the Manor, the Bishops of Salisbury. As a building it dominated the village and was the focal point for community activity:

'Religious belief affected human relationships, work, leisure, superstitions and all the manifold activities in which common attitudes find an echo. For successive generations, the church with its festivals, saints' days, processions, rituals, dramas and imagery, provided a pattern for the progress of each year and brought colour, music, light, hope and holiday into lives which would otherwise have been uniformly hard, monotonous and uncertain.'

Most, in the sixteenth century, believed God was intimately concerned with the minutest details of their daily lives, controlled as they were in their thoughts, speech and actions by the church courts.

Grotesque carved bosses indicate the powerful culture of pre-Christian beliefs and the sources of evil. Despite Christian teaching, the people hung on to their earlier spiritual symbols. These bosses would have been carved to protect the church from evil. They may have been caricatures of local people in the sixteenth century and display a medieval sense of humour.

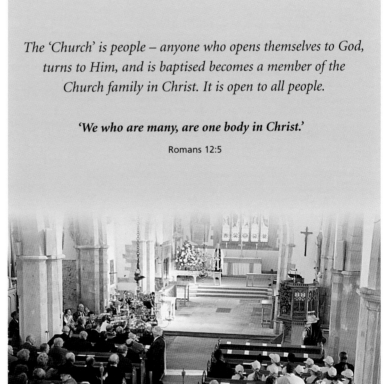

The 'Church' is people – anyone who opens themselves to God, turns to Him, and is baptised becomes a member of the Church family in Christ. It is open to all people.

'We who are many, are one body in Christ.'

Romans 12:5

Decoration: Holy Cross before the Reformation and 1534 Act of Supremacy, would have been a riot of colour, with painted stone and woodwork, murals, stained glass, lights, and highly-decorated altars, screens and statues. After the Reformation much of this, together with silver and vestments, was obliterated, confiscated, sold or hidden. The walls were whitewashed and scriptural texts, such as the Ten Commandments, the Creed and the Lord's Prayer, as well as Biblical scenes, were painted on them. A few remnants of the old decoration can be seen on some roof beams (see the stripes on the beam above the chancel arch, *top right*), on stonework by the Darrell Chapel *(right)* and chevrons round the chancel and other arches.

Medieval churches often had a fresco of St Christopher, carrying Christ over water, on the north wall so it would be the first thing people saw on entering through the main south door. It was thought that if a person caught a glimpse of him as they entered the church and offered a prayer they would be protected on their travels for the rest of the day. A St Christopher fresco was painted on the late-fourteenth century wall of the north aisle in Holy Cross but was in such a dilapidated state by 1891, it could not be preserved.

The pews and box pews

The medieval church had no seating apart from the stone seats against the walls for the elderly and infirm. As the Mass proceeded, the villagers stood or knelt on the beaten earth floors, which were covered in straw or litter. After the Reformation teaching became an important part of the new Book of Common Prayer service. Thus preaching long sermons, often three hours in length, brought a need for seating so wooden pew benches were put into churches, together with pulpits.

In 1698 permission was given for a gallery to be built on the west wall of Holy Cross to allow more seating. In 1788, as the congregation further increased, galleries were built over the north and south aisles.

Box pews had been put in Holy Cross by the beginning of the eighteenth century. The seats were bought by wealthy members of the community for their own and servants' use as a way of raising money for the upkeep of the church. The seats became appropriated to the family's house. They rapidly became a status symbol. Thus the Lord of the Manor and Patron (Richard Jones Esq. in c.1710) and his servants were in the chancel, while the parish seats for the poor were at the back of the church.

Seating plan c.1710

Notice the position of the pulpit, a three-decker, the way up to the rood loft, the tower entrance and staircase turret, the position of the font, with midwives beside it, the parish seats for the poor who couldn't pay, and the pay table where dues were collected.[3]

By 1779 Sir William and Lady Jones had appropriated further seats in the nave, but many of the increasingly wealthy tanners, brewers and other craftsmen in the village had their own seats too.

1 PULPIT
2 READING DESK
3 CLERK'S PEW
4 FONT
5 PAY DESK
6 PARISH SEATS
7 MIDWIVES' SEATS
8 WAY UP TO ROOD LOFT
9 RICHARD JONES Esq. (Manor)
10 SIR SEYMOUR PYLE (Axford)
11 VICARAGE PEW
12 FRANCIS POPHAM Esq. (Littlecote)
13 THOMAS BATSON Esq.
    (Parliament Piece)
14 HILLDROP
15 HENRY READ Esq. (Crowood)
16 HAILS COURT
17 STEPHEN BANKS
18 THE APPLEFORDS
19 MRS HILL

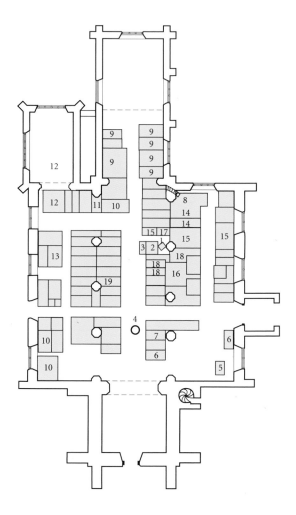

Seating plan c.1779:

Notice the pulpit, now moved to the north side of the chancel arch, the steps up to the singers' gallery by the north and south doors, the new outside opening to the tower staircase turret, the removal of the steps up to the rood loft, and the midwives' corner in the north-west of the church (see photo page 15).

The box pews kept out the draughts and dogs, but in 1891 the vicar, Harry Baber, complained at how dark they made the church, so they were taken out at the restoration then. Chairs were used until the present pews were put in, in 1910. The ones in the north-west and south-west corners were removed in 1986 to create a children's corner and a fellowship area.[4]

Chandeliers:

Each chandelier has twelve branches. The following people subscribed to the cost:

	£.	s.	d.
Col.Popham [Littlecote]	5.	5.	0
Will:Jones Esq [The Manor]	5.	5.	0
Thos:Batson Esq [Parliament Piece and Hilldrop Farm]	1.	1.	0
Rev.Ri:Garrard, Vicar		12.	6
Mr Benj:Symonds		10.	6
Mr Thos:Rawlinson		10.	6
Mr Bar:Staples		10.	6
etc.[5]			

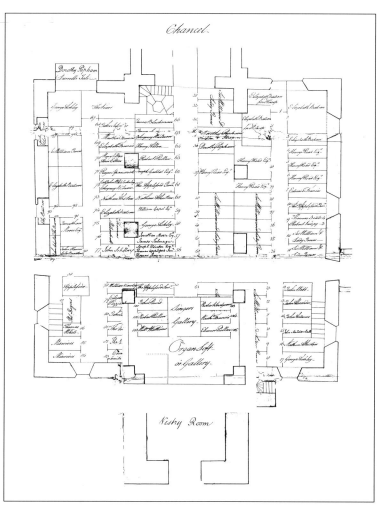

'Again Jesus spoke to them, saying:

I am the light of the world. Whoever follows Me will never walk in darkness but will have the Light of Life.'

John 8:12

Walk down the nave towards the chancel arch. →

THE CHANCEL ARCH AREA [6]

Under the thirteenth-century chancel arch Nuptial Masses and Marriages have always been celebrated. The wall above the archway would have been highly decorated with paintings. In front of the chancel step had been a rood screen and loft, dividing the people in the nave from the clergy in the chancel. It also kept animals out of the chancel. It was probably removed during the Reformation. Access was up some stairs which used to be on the north side of the St Helena Chapel, and through the doorway, now blocked up, which can be seen on the wall above the pulpit steps on your right. From the rood loft prayers were said and psalms sung.

A corbel, which formerly supported the screen, can be seen above the clergy seat on the left side of the chancel arch. It has been carved as a Green Man with leaves coming out of the mouth. These originated as pre-Christian representations of new life and re-birth. They are commonly found in churches all over Europe, and often as corbels supporting the rood screen.

Rood screens and lofts: Rood means the image of Christ on the Cross so rood screens are surmounted by this image, with the Virgin Mary on one side of Him and John the Evangelist on the other. People could look up to Christ, during the service.

Anglo-Saxon and Norman churches were undivided by rood screens but when Holy Cross was built in the thirteenth century, the screens had become common.

They had doors in them which were shut or locked to stop people and dogs entering the chancel, the domain of the clergy. They were usually intricately carved, coloured and guilded. Most were destroyed during the Reformation or in the Civil War.

Although the loft was narrow, prayers were said and psalms sung there and organs were often situated in them.

'I lift up my eyes to the hills – from where will my help come?

My help comes from the Lord, who made heaven and earth.'

Psalm 121:1-2

The Green Man: Carved Green Men, in a multitude of different forms, are commonly found across Europe, mainly in churches. Although they hark back to pre-Christian belief, their representation of creation and new birth links them to the Resurrection and new life in Christ, hence the corbel supporting the rood screen and crucifix.

They were attacked by early Christians as pagan, but then accepted as part of the link between nature and humanity. Repressed in the Reformation, they burst forth as a symbol of the fruits of learning in the Renaissance. Luther's work of the 1520s incorporated them, Michelangelo used them, as did Sir Christopher Wren in St Paul's Cathedral.

They appeared in art as well as sculpture, fitting well into the Baroque style.

The Green Men disappeared in the eighteenth and nineteenth centuries, though they are on the gates of Kew Gardens, built in 1843, and on the Houses of Parliament.

As the industrial era separated people from their environment, the Green Man died out.[6]

The beauty of the Kennet valley around Holy Cross is an ever-present reminder of the grace of our Creator God:

'In the beginning God created the heavens and the earth.

God saw everything He had made and indeed it was very good.'

Genesis 1:1, 31

The pulpit

The pulpit, was carved in oak in memory of Harry Baber, the vicar who oversaw the major restoration of the church in 1891. It was given by his grateful parishioners. It was limed in the 1960s, giving the wood its unusual appearance. Before 1891 a pulpit with a sounding board stood on the north side of the chancel arch *(right)*.

Pulpits only came into being when sermons became more common in the fifteenth century. By 1603 church-wardens were required to provide pulpits in their churches.

Pulpits: By the fifteenth century preaching had become general and in 1603 churchwardens were required to provide a pulpit in their church.

Originally, sermons were given standing in front of the altar, then at the west end of the chancel, then from rood lofts. Finally pulpits were used.

Jacobean pulpits were richly carved and had a sounding board above. Three-decker pulpits *(right)* became common, with the preacher in the upper deck, the reading clerk in the middle, from where the Bible and service were read, and the parish clerk's pew below. The Holy Cross seating plan of c.1710 (page 24), clearly shows a three-decker pulpit against the south-easternmost pillar of the nave.

Most pulpits are now positioned on the north side, with the lectern on the south, as in the c.1779 seating plan. A suggested reason is that the Gospel, being more important than the preaching, was read from the more important south side. This was changed in Holy Cross at the 1891 restoration, with the pulpit in its present position on the south side of the chancel arch.

God gives each of us gifts; one is interpretation of the Scriptures through the Holy Spirit, for preaching and teaching:

'And there are varieties of gifts, but the same Spirit…

To one is given through the Spirit the utterance of wisdom, and to another the utterance of knowledge according to the same Spirit…'

1 Corinthians 12: 4, 8

The parish clerk: The parish clerk would help the clergy to sing or say divine service, help the priest with house sacrament, ring bells, take charge of the goods of the church and keep the church keys.

It was also known for the parish clerk to administer corporal punishment to young people who misbehaved during services. Even in 1871, in Holy Cross, it was known for the sexton, who had taken over the duties of the parish clerk, to come to church armed with an ash-stick to be used during divine service to check the unruly.

The Meyricks

Two memorials by the pulpit are to Edward Meyrick, who became vicar of Ramsbury in 1785, and his son, Edward Graves Meyrick, who succeeded him as vicar in 1811. The father set up a school at the vicarage, which flourished and spread into two other large houses in Back Lane, Bodorgan, now Ramsbury Hill, and Parliament Piece. The son continued the school, which was attended, among others, by a nephew of Jane Austen, and John Moultrie, a friend of Keats.

The country parson: Edward Graves Meyrick was not only the vicar but also a magistrate, sportsman and farmer. Having many friends, he dined everywhere, loved his horses, greyhounds, and a hand of whist, visited his house in Harley Street, London, and frequently travelled abroad with his brother, Arthur.

At home, he tended his land, at Love's farm, and every Monday and some Saturdays sat on the bench in the Justice Room, near Holy Cross, or rode to sessions at Newbury, Devizes, Hungerford or Marlborough. These trips usually ended with dinner at a hostelry, and a little gambling after.

He, his wife, Myra, and their seven children became firm friends with Thomas Smith and

his family, who rented the Manor. Thus much interchange and dining ensued between the two families. Eight to ten horses in the vicarage stables allowed visiting friends, hunting or riding just for pleasure.

Myra was 'a woman of great character, beauty and intelligence' who also enjoyed coursing and hunting to the full.

Edward's brother, Arthur, ran the school while Myra undertook many of Edward's church duties. She arranged for people to take services when he was away and undertook all the little details to ensure a smooth relationship with the villagers. Despite his frequent absences, the church was always full.

Myra was griefstricken when he died in March 1839, but with seven children to care for, she spent no time nursing her sorrow. She and her family left Ramsbury in 1840 and although the school closed in 1851, Arthur's family stayed on in the village.

Henry, Edward and Myra's second son, recalls some of the village people in Holy Cross in his childhood in the 1820s:

'Joe Piper who made his boots, Mother Stag who kept bees, Old Smoker in his long smock frock, Tim March who could tickle a trout, and Miss Reason who churned the butter, Betty Minat who taught him to milk and Mother Pemberton who made her responses in so shrill a voice!'

It is not only clergy, but all who follow Christ, who are part of the royal priesthood, and thus called to love and serve Him in this world and play our part in growing the Church:

'But you are a chosen race, a royal priesthood, a holy nation, God's own people, in order that you may proclaim the mighty acts of Him who called you out of darkness into His marvellous light.'

1 Peter 2:9

The lectern

Two local families, the Waldrons of Marridge Hill, and the Rumbolls, who had a butcher's shop in the Square, donated the brass eagle lectern, after the 1891 restoration.

'The Word became flesh and lived among us.'

John 1:14

History: Before the Reformation the lectern was positioned in the chancel, behind the rood screen. It was used by the clergy to hold the service book.

The eagle is associated with the Gospel writer, John, who begins his Book thus:

'In the beginning was the Word, and the Word was with God, and the Word was God.'

John 1:1.

These words, together with the rest of the Scriptures, are read from the lectern and are metaphorically spread, by the soaring eagle, throughout the world. An eagle can also look unflinchingly into the heart of the sun, just as the words of the Bible are an unflinching revelation of God.

Incredibly, the Bible still speaks to us today in all the problems and joys of our daily lives, even though it is nearly 2000 years old. Reading it regularly brings a greater depth and meaning to life, as it reveals God's love and compassion for each one of us:

'Jesus said: It is written, One does not live by bread alone, but by every word that comes from the mouth of God.'

Matthew 4:4

'Indeed, the word of God is living and active, sharper than any two-edged sword, piercing until it divides soul from spirit, joints from marrow; it is able to judge the thoughts and intentions of the heart. And before Him no creature is hidden, but all are naked and laid bare to the eyes of the One to whom we must render an account.'

Hebrews 4:12-13

'You have seen … how I bore you on eagles' wings and brought you to Myself.'

Exodus 19:4

Cartouche memorial

Notice the fine example of a cartouche memorial on the wall behind the lectern, to Jonathan Knackstone, a farmer at Whittonditch. He 'was never known to murmur [complain] though deprived by Nature of the Organs of Hearing and Speaking.' He died in 1745, aged 63.

Doran Webb, who wrote *The History of the Hundred of Ramsbury, Part 1* in 1890, suggests that 'men being such born grumblers, in his opinion, it was astonishing that even a dumb man (whose misfortunes would have afforded him some excuse in the matter)…' had not complained!

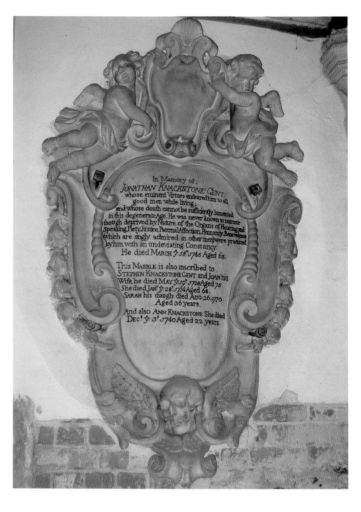

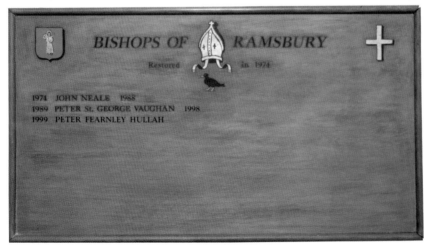

Above the Bishop's stall is the list of the Bishops of Ramsbury since 1974.

The organ

The fine organ was given by Miss Read of Crowood House, in 1838. It was erected at the west end of the church, but in 1891 it was moved to its present position, when additions were made to it. In 1960, and again in 1981, it was renovated.

The organ: Although the organ was given to the church in 1838, it is thought the pipework could have been made about 50 years earlier, possibly by George Pike England. It was a small one-manual organ of eight stops and a pedal bourdon.

By 1960 the organ was in poor condition, full of dirt, pipes collapsing and much of the mechanical action broken or not working. By good fortune, the composer and organist, Anthony Scott, who also delighted in repairing and restoring organs, was asked, and agreed, to help.

He set to work with enthusiasm and restored the organ as an instrument not only for normal service use but also for a wider repertory, particularly music of the seventeenth and eighteenth centuries. The work was paid for by Miss Priscilla Ashley, in memory of her family who had been leading brewers and tanners in the village over a number of centuries.

The case, described by Pevsner as a 'very pretty Gothick piece', was painted in grey, red and gold at the suggestion of Mrs Gerald Finzi, wife of the composer, who lived locally.[7]

The organ has been successfully broadcast on several occasions, most recently at the BBC One Easter Morning service, 23 April 2000.

Music in churches: Organs were first used in churches from the tenth century. By the thirteenth century many large parish churches had them, possibly including Holy Cross, especially as it was used for ordination services by the Bishops of Salisbury. They were in smaller churches by the fifteenth century. Most were situated in the rood loft but the Reformation brought the destruction of the rood screen and loft, along with the organs. The Puritans, especially through the Commonwealth, campaigned against the use of organs or any music in worship.

From the late seventeenth century to the mid-nineteenth century music was reintroduced and the liturgy sung, so galleries at the west end of churches were built for musicians and singers. The gallery at Holy Cross was built right across the west end of the church in 1698-9. It was accessed by stairs on the north and south walls and stretched from the tower arch to the nearest pillars in the nave, from the west. The central section was reserved for the singers. The musicians played a variety of instruments such as the bassoon, viol, hautboy (oboe), clarinet, bass fiddle, violincello, serpent and flute.

Hymns were introduced in the nineteenth century, with the book of Ancient and Modern Hymns published in 1861. When the hymns and psalms were sung, the congregation turned round to face the musicians and singers in the gallery.

By the eighteenth century organs came back into churches and were usually put in the west end gallery. This is where the Holy Cross organ was before the 1891 restoration, when it was moved to its present position and the gallery demolished.

The acoustics of Holy Cross are good so a number of concerts have been held in the church to raise funds for charities or church repairs. Moura Lympany, The Scholars, and Peter Katin have performed here. To aid recent repairs, Music in Country Churches brought the Belcea Quartet and the pianist, Maria João Pires to Holy Cross on 9 and 10 July 1999, the latter in the presence of His Royal Highness, the Prince of Wales. Musicians from the Chetham School of Music played at the BBC One Easter 2000 service, including the violinist, Jennifer Pike, who became BBC Young Musician of the Year 2002 at the age of 14.

For many, music brings an added dimension to worship; it can lift us out of the ordinary into a knowledge of the 'Otherness' of God:

'Be filled with the Spirit, as you sing psalms and hymns and spiritual songs among yourselves, singing and making melody to the Lord in your hearts, giving thanks to God the Father at all times and for everything in the name of our Lord Jesus Christ.'

Ephesians 5:19

'O for a thousand tongues to sing my great Redeemer's praise, the glories of my God and King, the triumphs of His grace!'

Charles Wesley (1707-88)

Pass through the curtained opening by the organ into the Darrell Chapel and look behind the organ at the stained glass window. →

ST KATHARINE'S CHAPEL [7]

The remains of two intricately carved (crocketted) pinnacles, one on either side of the window behind the organ, suggest that this was possibly the place where the altar to St Katharine the Virgin was consecrated in 1453. The table tomb, which now stands on the north wall of the Darrell Chapel, may have stood below the window before the organ was placed there.

The stained glass, depicting St Paul with his sword, and St Timothy with his quill pen, was placed in memory of the Revd Arthur Meyrick (brother of Edward Graves Meyrick), who died in 1855, and his wife, Mary Ann, who died in 1866.

History: According to the Bishops' Registers, the Bishop of Salisbury consecrated an altar dedicated to St Katharine in the north part of the church in 1453.[8]

The window behind the organ would have been in the north transept of the cruciform church in the early fourteenth century, before the aisles were extended later that century (see page 3).

The pillar nearest the organ has the remains of what seems to be the base of an arch springing from it, suggesting this area was separated from the body of the church, so it may have been a side chapel.

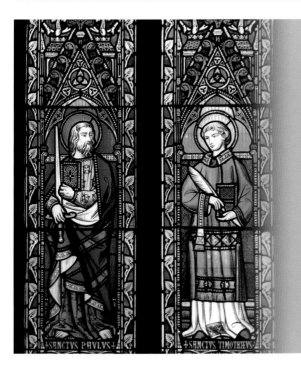

Some advice from Paul's second letter to Timothy:

'If we have died with Him, we will also live with Him;

if we endure we will also reign with Him;

if we deny Him, He will also deny us;

if we are faithless, He remains faithful –

for He cannot deny Himself.'

2 Timothy 2:11-13

Now turn back into the Darrell Chapel.→

THE DARRELL CHAPEL [8]

Added to the church in the early fifteenth century, as a chantry and Lady Chapel (dedicated to the Virgin Mary), by the Calston family of Littlecote, the chapel houses the Purbeck 'marble' table tomb attributed to William Darrell and his wife, Elizabeth, daughter and heiress of Thomas Calston. William was Sub-Treasurer of England under Richard II, and Sheriff of Wiltshire in the reigns of Henry V and VI. Recent investigations indicate this was a burial tomb rather than simply a memorial one. The position of the tomb, with its brasses, facing the altar and the east was of great importance for the hope of resurrection and new life.

The mutilated tomb, with canopy, against the north wall is possibly that of Sir George Darrell, son of William. The plain altar tomb opposite may be of his son, Sir Edward Darrell, Vice-Chamberlain to Henry VIII, who died in 1528.

The brasses were possibly removed, with others in the church, during the Civil War.

The floor tiles are Victorian Meissen.

The stone niches beside the east window and in the north-east corner would probably have held statues in pre-Reformation times, including one of the Virgin Mary as this was a Lady Chapel.

Notice the piscina in the south wall. Unlike the other piscinas in the church, this one has a credence shelf in it on which the sacred Communion vessels were placed.

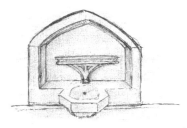

The lost brasses: Brasses, made of a copper-zinc mix, were commonly used on tombs from the thirteenth to seventeenth centuries, but were often stolen to use the metal for other purposes.

The **central tomb** brasses, dated c.1460, depict a man in armour, bare-headed, probably with a rolled hairstyle, a sword in his left hand and a dog at his feet. His wife is in a gown and mitre head-dress. Above their heads are the Holy Trinity in the centre, the kneeling Virgin with mouth scroll on the right and a further religious group on the left.

Above the religious groups are three shields, each surmounted with a helm and crest. The centre crest is a Saracen's head in profile, on the right is a bird and on the left an arm with the hand grasping a short sword or dagger. Six shields complete the brasses.

The table tomb, also of Purbeck 'marble', on the north wall of the chapel, has a badly mutilated canopy but on the back panel are indents of three people kneeling at prayer desks with a long narrow foot inscription below. In the centre is a man with shoulder-length hair, probably in armour. Behind him is a wife in pedimental head-dress, and possibly three daughters standing behind her. Facing the man is a second wife, again in pedimental head-dress, and possibly three daughters behind her.

Above them, in the centre is a Holy Trinity, with a shield on either side, one surmounted by the Saracen's head and crest, the other by an arm grasping a short sword or dagger.

Dated c.1500, the kneeling position for effigies was common in the sixteenth century.[9]

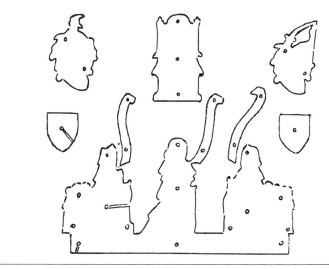

Tombs may remind us of loved ones in our lives who have died:

'Be gentle with the one who walks with grief.

If it is you, be gentle with yourself.

Swiftly forgive; walk slowly, pausing often.

Take time, be gentle as you walk with grief.'

Celtic Night Prayer,
Northumbrian Community

The Darrell family: William Darrell was the younger son of Sir William Darrell of Sessay, Yorkshire. He married Elizabeth, the daughter and heiress of Thomas Calston, of Littlecote, and Joan, his wife, daughter and co-heir of Thomas Chelrey of Childrey, Berkshire.

Their son, Sir George Darrell, had two wives, Margaret, daughter of John, first Lord Stourton, and Jane, daughter of Sir William Hawte, of Shelvingbourne, Kent. By his first wife he had three daughters. One married John Seymour of Wolfhall, Queen Jane Seymour's family. By his second wife he had a son, Sir Edward Darrell, who bequeathed money for daily Masses to be said in the chapel for the souls of his family. His great-grandson was the notorious 'Wild' William Darrell who reputedly had a baby burnt to death at Littlecote. 'Wild' Darrell met an untimely death and was buried at Kintbury Church in 1589.

Family tree: Darrell

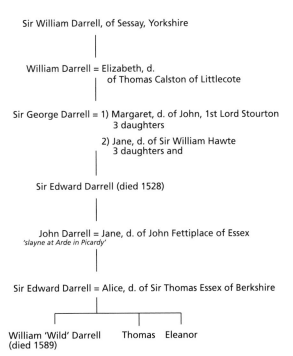

Sir William Darrell, of Sessay, Yorkshire

William Darrell = Elizabeth, d. of Thomas Calston of Littlecote

Sir George Darrell = 1) Margaret, d. of John, 1st Lord Stourton
3 daughters

2) Jane, d. of Sir William Hawte
3 daughters and

Sir Edward Darrell (died 1528)

John Darrell = Jane, d. of John Fettiplace of Essex
'slayne at Arde in Picardy'

Sir Edward Darrell = Alice, d. of Sir Thomas Essex of Berkshire

William 'Wild' Darrell (died 1589)   Thomas   Eleanor

Leave the Darrell Chapel as you entered and go back to the chancel arch and into the chancel. →

THE CHANCEL [9]

You may notice as you look back down the nave that the chancel and nave are very slightly out of alignment. This is a common occurrence in churches and various suggestions for it are: an error in building work; as a distraction to the devil; or a symbolic representation of Christ's head leaning to one side on the cross. Remember that medieval people still clung to their old pre-Christian beliefs even while following the Christian faith.

Dating from the thirteenth century, the chancel is the oldest part of the present church. It is a long one and may have been the site of the original Anglo-Saxon cathedral minster. In 1891 the footings of a wall, running parallel to the chancel and about 3 feet to the south of it, were discovered. It is thought they were part of the Anglo-Saxon cathedral.

Just inside the chancel are two thirteenth-century side arch niches, with bell capitols, which may have been where priests sat during services.

The chancel was the domain of the priests, who had their own entrance, seen here in the door on the south side. Notice the fifteenth-century false arcade of arches, or windows, with a door, possibly an earlier priest's door, on the north wall. The present windows were also inserted in the fifteenth century, but the stained glass is 1907.

The oak choir stalls, given by Baroness Burdett-Coutts (page 50) in 1891, replaced box pews for the family at the Manor. There were two rows of stalls on each side, but one row was removed to widen access to the sanctuary. The oak credence tables and altar table were also given after the 1891 restoration. The oak was limed in the 1960s.

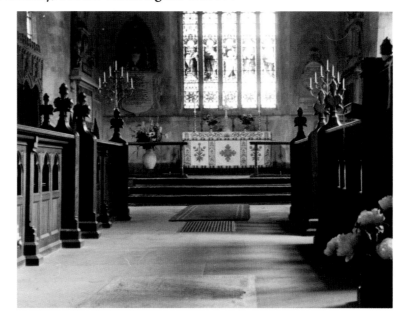

The mutilated canopied altar-tomb of Purbeck 'marble', possibly for William York of Hilldrop, a homestead north of the village, is late fifteenth century. A visitor, Captain Symonds, in 1644 records that the brasses had already gone from the tomb by then. It may have served the purpose of an Easter sepulchre. Notice the

carved twisted pillars on the left and the niche for an image on the right, also the twisted fan vaulting on the roof of the tomb.

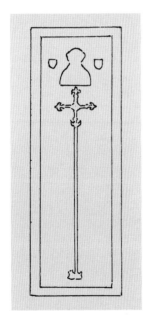

Among the various memorial stones on the chancel floor is one, at the foot of the sanctuary steps, to William de St John, Prebend of Ramsbury from 1320-22. This was the normal position for the memorial to the person who was most important in the building of the church, and in particular the chancel. The incised inscription round the edge of the stone is in Norman French, in separate Lombardic capitals between fillets, as follows:

SOUTZ . CESTE . PERE . LETTERE . OV . LATON . GIST. WILLM . LA . SEINT . JOHN . DE . RAMM . ESBVRY . PERSONE . ET . FER . POR . SA . ALME . PRIER . OR . ASON . QARANT . JOYRS . ASSVRON . DE . P'DON .

'Under this stone lettered with brass lies William de Saint John, Parson of Rammesbury and to make [people] say a prayer for his soul we assure [them] forty days of pardon.'

The ceiling of the chancel is Georgian and covers a much older barrel-vaulted roof. When the Georgian ceiling was constructed it unfortunately covered the top of the east window.

Where was the Anglo-Saxon cathedral minster?

Was it under the chancel, or adjacent to it, or under another part of the present church?

- The footings of a wall 3 feet to the south of and parallel to the chancel was discovered in the 1891 restoration work.
- The medieval church builders tended to construct the first part of a new church beside an earlier one so services could continue in the old church. Then, when built, the new chancel was used and probably the old one demolished and used as building stone for the rest of the church. Did this happen here?
- Were the footings the north wall of the Anglo-Saxon church?
- Alternatively, the footings could have been the south wall of the Anglo-Saxon church, which then extended under the present chancel.
- The Anglo-Saxon and Norman builders were very accurate, the medieval ones less so. Is it possible the misalignment between the chancel and nave is because the medieval builders constructed the chancel on the lines of the old Anglo-Saxon cathedral minster, but then attached the nave at a slight angle as there were no underlying foundations to guide them?
- Why were no indications of the old cathedral minster found in 1891 when the floor of the main body of the church was taken up down to bare earth in order to construct a waterproof flooring? The builders had found and excavated the footings and the Anglo-Saxon stones so they must have been aware that other footings could have been somewhere near. So perhaps they

didn't find any under the rest of the present church.

We won't know unless further research is carried out.

Chantries: A chantry was a medieval ecclesiastical endowment (payment) for keeping priests to say Mass for the soul of someone who had died. Chapels were often provided for the use of a chantry, and held the tomb of the founder and his family. In the fifteenth century chantries were founded by social guilds for religious and philanthropic purposes, and became common.

In 1459 William York of Hilldrop was granted a licence 'to found a chantry of one chaplain to celebrate divine service daily in honour of the Holy Trinity at the altar of St Mary the Virgin in the church of Holy Cross, Ramesbury [sic],…for the souls of Nicholas Wootton, John York, father of the said William, and Agnes, sometime wife of William [and daughter of Nicholas] and for the good estate of the King and William and all others who hold the chantry and for their souls after death, and to instruct in the rudiments of grammar without payment any poor and indigent scholars flocking to the town from any parts of the realm.'[10]

Estates in Purton and elsewhere,

and several cottages in Ramsbury, were given to endow the chantry, while the right to nominate the chaplain passed with Hilldrop manor. In 1535, out of the annual chantry income of £8.2s.0d., the Bishop of Salisbury received 19d., the Abbot of Glastonbury 3s.4d. and the poor 1s.8d.

By 1547 the chantry had been dissolved, without licence, and later sold. All chantries were dissolved by Edward VI.

Endowments for lamps to be burnt before the reserved sacrament in churches, were also given. In 1549 an annual sum of 2s. was obtained from land called 'le lampelande', now Lamplands, across the river, 'to the light in the parish church of Ramesbury.'[11]

Lamplands

The Easter sepulchre: The position of the tomb on the north wall of the chancel, near the sanctuary, suggests it may have been an Easter sepulchre. On Good Friday, in medieval times, the Host and an altar crucifix were placed in the sepulchre and watched day and night until they were removed, with great festival, to the high altar very early on Easter Sunday morning, thus signifying Christ's burial in and resurrection from the tomb.

At other times, the chantry priest would possibly have sat on the left of the tomb, looking between the pillars towards the image, maybe of the Virgin Mary, opposite him, as he said Mass.

The indents of former brasses on this canopied altar-tomb indicate a kneeling civilian with shoulder-length hair, and with a scroll issuing from his hands to the Holy Trinity. A foot inscription and two shields complete the composition.

Good Friday is a day of remembering Jesus' overwhelming love for each one of us. In suffering and dying, He gave His life so that all people can share in the resurrection and new life He offers to us, through His Holy Spirit, both here and now and after we die.

All He asks of us is to set aside our old way of life, where we ignore Him, and turn instead to a new life with Him, full of richness and meaning. It is our free choice.

It is only when He is in the centre of our lives, in our hearts, that we can be set free – from worry, anxiety, despair, anger - and learn to love as He loves us.

'Today, if you hear His voice, do not harden your hearts.' Hebrews 4:7

Who is Jesus?
He was born in Bethlehem over 2000 years ago.
During His first thirty years He shared the daily life and work of an ordinary home.
For the next three years He went about teaching small groups and healing sick and troubled people in villages, in the fields and by the lakeside.
He called twelve ordinary people to be His helpers.
He had no money.
He never owned His own home.
He wrote no books.
He commanded no army.
He wielded no political power.
During His life He never travelled more than two hundred miles in any direction.
He was executed by being nailed to a cross, at the age of 33.
When He was dead, He was laid in a borrowed grave, through the pity of a friend.
Three days later, He rose to new life and appeared to His friends, transforming them from frightened, defeated men to fearless and joyful messengers. All of them, apart from John, were tortured and killed for speaking of their total belief in Him as the Son of God and in His resurrection.
No one else has affected the lives of men and women on earth as much as that
One Solitary Life.

Easter joy of the resurrection

'I am the resurrection and the life. Those who believe in Me, even though they die, will live, and everyone who lives and believes in Me will never die.'

John 11:25.

Understanding the supreme unconditional love of God through Christ's death and resurrection, helps us to realise that however much we may do or say wrong things, if we believe in Him, and say we are sorry, we are forgiven. We can place the heavy burden of our wrong doings and problems at the foot of the cross. The guilt is acknowledged, forgiven and lifted from us. He sets us free.

'Thine be the glory, risen, conquering Son, endless is the victory Thou o'er death hast won.' Edmond Budry (1854-1932)

William de St John, Prebend of Ramsbury 1320-22:
On the floor in the centre of the chancel, with the end slightly covered by the sanctuary steps, is a 'Unio' Purbeck 'marble' slab. On it are the indents of the bust of a priest, over a cross with fleur-de-lys ends and an undecorated stem rising from the back of a small animal. Two small shields of arms are on either side of the bust.

The lettering around the stone is as on page 42. It was unusual to mention brass lettering on memorials so the words 'cest pere lettere ov laton', confirming that the stone was inlaid with letters of laton, the medieval word for brass, are probably unique.

The small animal at the base of

the cross may have been the trademark of the workshop. A.G.Sadler, in his book *The Indents of the Lost Monumental Brasses of Wiltshire* says: 'Two early workshops, both almost certainly in London, used "Unio" and "ordinary" Purbeck respectively. The "Unio" workshop produced a distinctive form of simple cross and demi-figure, usually with separate Lombardic letters without fillets and a little animal at the foot of the stem, which is something of a trademark.'

Now approach the most holy part of the church, the sanctuary. It is a place of stillness in the presence of God. →

THE SANCTUARY [10]

You may wish to lay before God your concerns, your love
and trust, and even your self; simply 'be' in His presence
and make a sanctuary for Him in your own heart and life.

'Be still,

for the presence of the Lord, the Holy One is here;

come bow before Him now with reverence and fear;

in Him no sin is found –

we stand on holy ground.

Be still,

for the presence of the Lord, the Holy One, is here.'

David J. Evans

The altar is the holy heart of the church. It is a wooden table at which the shared meal of the Eucharist is prepared. It was given by Samuel Jones of Ramsbury Manor in 1685, but the table top is a later replacement.

The two piscinas, on the north and south walls, are thirteenth century. The south wall piscina, now partly covered by the tomb, has Purbeck 'marble' columns and trefoiled heads. Beside it is a stone bench which may have been a sedilia where assisting clergy would have sat.

The memorials in the sanctuary are in memory of the Jones and Burdett families, who owned Ramsbury Manor from 1680-1951. The reclining figure is of Sir William Jones (1631-82), Attorney-General to Charles II. In 1800 the Manor passed to Sir Francis Burdett, 5th Baronet, and a Member of Parliament, who inherited it from his aunt, Elizabeth Langham Jones. His memorial, with his wife, a daughter of Sir Thomas Coutts, the banker, is on the right of the east window.

It was their youngest daughter, Angela, who inherited the Coutts fortune and through her philanthropic work was created the first woman Baroness in her own right, taking the title Baroness Angela Burdett-Coutts. She gave £1000 towards the £6000 needed for the 1891 restoration work on the church, and donated the oak (now limed) choir stalls and clergy reading desks. She is buried in Westminster Abbey.

The altar rails were given in memory of Admiral Hyde Parker, churchwarden from 1930 to 1950.

The east window stained glass is in memory of Sir Francis Burdett, the 7th Baronet, who died in 1892. He paid for the restoration of the chancel in 1891.

The kneelers were designed by Mrs Marjorie Howe and stitched by a team of local people, together with those in the nave, in the 1970s, led by Mrs Marian Davies, wife of the vicar, the Revd 'Jack' Davies.

The wooden cross was made from part of the ancient elm tree which formerly stood in the centre of the village, at the Square. Over 300 years old, it died in 1986 and was replaced by an English oak. The cross was carved in 1995 by Michael Franklin. A brass cross is used for services, together with two brass candlesticks donated in 1995 in memory of Christopher Eliot-Cohen, of Hilldrop.

The pair of seven-light candelabra were presented by Mary and Katharine Meyrick in 1906.

Extract taken from the song "Be Still" by David J Evans Copyright© 1986 Thankyou Music*

The Eucharist (meaning 'thanksgiving') along with Baptism, is one of the two sacraments instituted by Jesus Himself. It is central to the Christian faith, and we receive it in memory of Him and His death and resurrection for us. As He and the disciples gathered in an upper room in Jerusalem for their last supper together before His death, 'Jesus took a loaf of bread and, after blessing it, He broke it and gave it to the disciples, and said "Take, eat; this is My body." Later, after they had eaten supper, He took a cup of wine, and after giving thanks He gave it to them, saying: "Drink from it, all of you for this is My blood of the covenant [relationship with God], which is poured out for many for the forgiveness of sins."' (Matthew 26:26-28)

As we reach out and accept the bread and wine, we make a conscious act of taking into our souls and bodies the love of Christ. Our sins are forgiven and we can share in His glorious resurrection:

'The Lord God will wipe away the tears from all faces.'

Isaiah 25:8

LOVE

'Love bade me welcome: yet my soul drew back,
Guiltie of dust and sinne.
But quick-ey'd Love, observing me grow slack
From my first entrance in,
Drew nearer to me, sweetly questioning,
If I lack'd any thing.

A guest, I answer'd, worthy to be here:
Love said, You shall be he.
I the unkinde, ungrateful? Ah my deare,
I cannot look on thee.
Love took my hand, and smiling did reply,
Who made the eyes but I?

Truth, Lord, but I have marr'd them: let my shame
Go where it doth deserve.
And know you not, sayes Love, who bore the blame?
My deare, then I will serve.
You must sit down, sayes Love, and taste my meat;
So I did sit and eat.'

George Herbert (1593-1633)

The altar: In Anglo-Saxon churches the altar was most often placed to the west of the chancel arch, but in the late Anglo-Saxon period it was moved to just east of the arch. In medieval times it moved again, either to the centre of the chancel or the east end, but not against the east wall. The east was chosen so the priest would symbolically be facing the rising sun, with his back to the congregation.

'The glory of the Lord coming from the east;' Ezekiel 43:2.

When the altar was in the centre of the chancel, the people tended to behave in an irreverent way while receiving communion, so Archbishop Laud (1573-1645) used his influence to have the altar moved to the east end, with altar rails erected for people to kneel at to receive communion. The rails also served to keep dogs away from the sanctuary. The imposing altar rails in Holy Cross, before the 1891 restoration, were replaced by oak ones in the 1950s.

By the eleventh century an altar was often also set up in the nave because the people were not allowed into the choir and sanctuary.

Altars were of stone until the Reformation when they were replaced with more easily movable wooden tables. The Holy Cross high altar table was given by Samuel Jones, of the Manor, in 1685. Various beautifully embroidered traditional altar frontals are used throughout the Church year.

Piscinas: Having two piscinas in the sanctuary is unusual and only occurred at the end of the twelfth and beginning of the thirteenth centuries, so their presence helps to date the church. One piscina, that on the south side, would have been used to dispose of the remaining consecrated wine after the Eucharist, hence the drainage hole going straight down in the centre onto the consecrated foundations. The piscina on the north side would have been used by the priest to wash his hands, hence the drain goes outwards at the back of the bowl, taking the dirty water away from the consecrated building. The water was probably poured over the priest's hands by a servitor, because the piscina is too shallow for his hands to have been immersed.

By the end of the thirteenth century, the priests had taken to consuming the remaining consecrated wine, so only one piscina was required, for washing.

Ramsbury Manor and Sir William Jones: In 1075 the Manor of Ramsbury passed from the Bishops of Ramsbury to the Bishops of Salisbury. From them, in 1545, during the Reformation, it was granted to Edward Seymour, later Duke of Somerset, the Lord Protector. Thus the link between the Manor and the Bishopric was severed after 600 years.

The esteem with which the Bishops of Salisbury regarded the beautiful park and 'palace' at Ramsbury extended to the church, which was praised, in 1538, by Leland, a writer and traveller, as 'a faire, and large olde churche.'

Following Edward Seymour's execution in 1552, the Manor was given to William Herbert, 1st Earl of Pembroke, of Wilton House, near Salisbury. It stayed in that family until the 7th Earl, who had become impoverished, sold it in 1676 to a consortium headed by Henry Powle, the Speaker of the House of Commons. They asset stripped it, and in 1680 sold the Manor house, remaining rents and about 700 acres to Sir William Jones *(below)*.

Renowned as the 'greatest lawyer in England, and a very wise man', Sir William was appointed Attorney-General to Charles II. He directed the prosecution in the Titus Oates' Plot in 1678, and entered Parliament in 1680. He pulled down the old Manor house and began building the present one but died, in 1682, before it was completed.

His funeral expenses came to £878 and the lush memorial to him cost £260, of which the stonework cost £200, the ironwork (railings, now gone) £36, and the Herald painting £24.

His pose of reclining on an elbow was common in the seventeenth century for effigies.

Sir Francis Burdett, 5th Baronet, MP: Sir Francis inherited great estates at Foremark, in Derbyshire, and in Berkshire, on his grandfather's death in 1797, so when he also inherited the Ramsbury estates from his aunt, Elizabeth Langham Jones, in 1800, he became a very wealthy young man. On entering Parliament he was rich enough to stand as an independent and could speak out against the

injustices of the time. This angered the political leaders, who had him imprisoned twice for challenging them, but it endeared him to the people, who dubbed him 'England's Glory' and 'Westminster's Pride'. His greatest achievement was helping to get the 1832 Reform Bill through Parliament, which gave voting rights to a much greater percentage of the population. He was noted in the House for his 'tall patrician figure with gentle bearing, mild eye, and serene bare brow.'

Sir Francis married Sophia, one of the 'three graces', daughters of Thomas Coutts, the banker. They were not suited so the marriage was frequently stormy. After Sophia's mother died, her father married Harriet Mellon, an actress, and left her the Coutt's fortune on his death. However, Harriet was an astute business lady and decided upon Angela, youngest daughter of Sir Francis and Sophia, as the one to inherit the Coutt's money. A friend of Charles Dickens, Angela

undertook much philanthropic work and became known as 'Queen of the Poor'. She was created the first woman Baroness in her own right, by Queen Victoria. She died in 1906, aged 91, and was buried in Westminster Abbey.

Sir Francis and Sophia died within a few days of each other and were buried together on 31 January 1844 in the crypt tomb under the sanctuary. The baronetcy ceased in 1951 with the death of the 8th Baronet, also Sir Francis, as he had no male heirs.

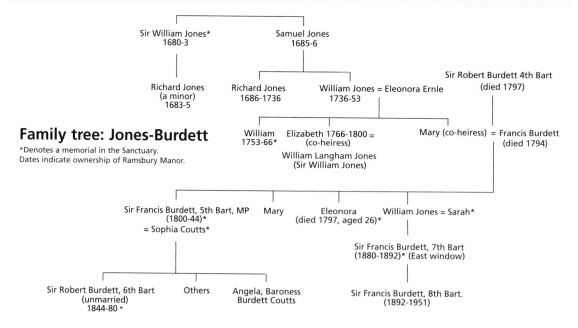

Family tree: Jones-Burdett

*Denotes a memorial in the Sanctuary.
Dates indicate ownership of Ramsbury Manor.

Sir William Jones* 1680-3
Samuel Jones 1685-6
Richard Jones (a minor) 1683-5
Richard Jones 1686-1736
William Jones = Eleonora Ernle 1736-53
Sir Robert Burdett 4th Bart (died 1797)
William 1753-66*
Elizabeth 1766-1800 = (co-heiress) William Langham Jones (Sir William Jones)
Mary (co-heiress) = Francis Burdett (died 1794)
Sir Francis Burdett, 5th Bart, MP (1800-44)* = Sophia Coutts*
Mary
Eleonora (died 1797, aged 26)*
William Jones = Sarah*
Sir Francis Burdett, 7th Bart (1880-1892)* (East window)
Sir Robert Burdett, 6th Bart (unmarried) 1844-80 *
Others
Angela, Baroness Burdett Coutts
Sir Francis Burdett, 8th Bart. (1892-1951)

The East window

The stained glass, put up in memory of Sir Francis Burdett, the seventh baronet, depicts the four evangelists, Matthew, Mark, Luke and John, each holding their Gospel books, standing on either side of Jesus. He is shown as the Good Shepherd, carrying one of His lambs. The dove, representing the Holy Spirit, is above Him, and through the tracery at the top of the window are lilies. As well as being a symbol of the Virgin Mary, lilies also depict Jesus' love for us, His Church.

Along the bottom are images of oak leaves for strength, durability, faith and endurance, a pomegranate bursting with seeds of fertility and bounty, a lily for love, and a white rose for purity and perfect beauty. Below Christ are the letters *ihc* from the first two and last letters of the Greek for Jesus – IHCOYC, surrounded by the fruits of the vine.

God is love – unconditional, always there for us, every moment of our lives, to eternity:

'As the Father has loved Me, so I have loved you; abide in My love.'

John 15:9

'And remember, I am with you always, to the end of the age.'

Matthew 28:20

The King of love my Shepherd is,
whose goodness faileth never;
I nothing lack if I am His
And He is mine for ever.

Where streams of living water flow
My ransomed soul He leadeth,
And where the verdant pastures grow
With food celestial feedeth.

Perverse and foolish oft I strayed;
But yet in love He sought me,
And on His shoulder gently laid,
And home rejoicing brought me.

In death's dark vale I fear no ill
With Thee, dear Lord, beside me;
Thy rod and staff my comfort still,
Thy cross before to guide me.

Thou spread'st a table in my sight;
Thy unction grace bestoweth;
And O what transport of delight
From Thy pure chalice floweth!

And so through all the length of days
Thy goodness faileth never.
Good Shepherd, may I sing Thy praise
within Thy house for ever.

Henry William Baker (1821-77) after Psalm 23.

TO THE GLORY OF GOD & IN LOVING MEMORY OF FRANCIS BURDETT 7TH BART THIS WINDOW ERECTED BY HIS SORROWING WIFE MARY DOROTHY & CHILDREN CLARE MAUD FRANCIS & MAUD BORN MARCH 23 1813 FELL ASLEEP MAY 31 1892

Symbols of Jesus: Early Christians used initials for Jesus as they considered it irreverent to write sacred names at length. The letters **ihc** were later translated into the Latin form **ihs**. Popularised in the fifteenth century, ihs has taken on other meanings, such as *Iesus, Hominum Salvator* (Jesus, Saviour of Humankind). Ihc appears on the East window below Jesus, and ihs on the front of the altar in the St Helena Chapel.

Along with ihc or ihs, is another sacred monogram, the Chi Rho . It stands for 'Christ' from the Greek word for Christ - XPICTOC. The Chi Rho was adopted by the Roman Emperor, Constantine. In AD 312 he invaded Italy, after declaring war on the then Emperor, Maxentius. Before battle he had a vision of the Chi Rho and the words 'By this sign you will conquer', with Jesus telling him to put the sign on his military standards. He did so and went on to defeat Maxentius, despite overwhelming odds.

Following his victory, Constantine declared Christianity the state religion and thus it spread throughout the Roman Empire, including Britain.

The letters INRI almost always appear above the crucified Christ, as on the crucifix above the pulpit steps. This stands for 'Iesus Nazarenus Rex Iudaeorum', the Latin for 'Jesus of Nazareth, King of the Jews'. They were the words, in Aramaic, Greek and Latin, which Pontius Pilate had inscribed and fastened to the Cross. (John 19:19-22)

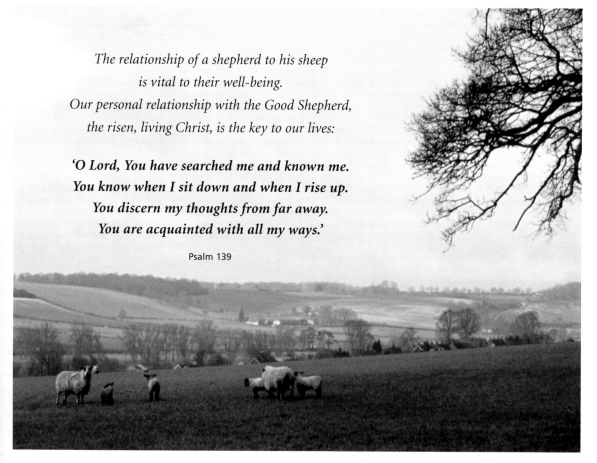

The relationship of a shepherd to his sheep
is vital to their well-being.
Our personal relationship with the Good Shepherd,
the risen, living Christ, is the key to our lives:

'O Lord, You have searched me and known me.
You know when I sit down and when I rise up.
You discern my thoughts from far away.
You are acquainted with all my ways.'

Psalm 139

53

Turning from the sanctuary, retrace your steps down the chancel, past the pulpit, and through the screen on the left to enter the St Helena Chapel. →

ST HELENA CHAPEL [11]

This chapel, which has taken over the role of a Lady Chapel, was probably built as a transept. In the later fourteenth century the north and south aisles were widened to incorporate the transepts (see page 3). The east window was inserted in the fifteenth century but the stained glass is dated 1861.

Notice the aumbry, a small cupboard, on the left, with a lamp over it, in which the Sacrament is kept to take to sick parishioners in their homes. Holy oils, blessed by the Bishop of Salisbury on Maundy Thursday, and used for anointing, are also kept in the aumbry. A piscina is in the south wall.

The carved wooden screen was placed around the altar to protect the candles from draughts. The screen on your left is in memory of John Henry Lawrence, churchwarden from 1914-36. Other furnishings, including the altar, were given by Mrs Florence Woolland and Mr and Mrs William Mills.

The limed-oak prayer desk, perhaps originally designed as a litany desk, was given in memory of Moses Woolland (died 1919). It has two angels carved on it which have a personal link with the present Bishop of Salisbury (see page 58). The kneelers have been made by Liz McIndoe and friends.

St Helena (c.250-330): The mother of the Roman Emperor, Constantine the Great, she was born in Asia Minor, the daughter of an innkeeper. In or about AD 270 she married a Roman general, who became Emperor, and Constantine was born in 274.

When he became Emperor in 306, he brought his mother to Rome where, in about 312, she became a devout Christian.

In 327 Constantine sent her to Jerusalem on a pilgrimage, where she was present when Christ's cross was found. She sent three of the nails back to her son and had a basilica built on the Mount of Olives.

It is fitting that in a church dedicated to the Holy Cross, this chapel is dedicated to St Helena.

The Annunciation: Mary's response to the angel Gabriel's message that she had been chosen by God to be the mother of Christ, whatever it cost her, was:

'Here I am, the servant of the Lord; let it be with me according to Your word.' Luke 1:38

Mary's obedience to the will of God is an example to us all. Following God's will for us brings joy, as Mary shows in her song of praise – the Magnificat:

*'My soul magnifies the Lord,
and my spirit rejoices in God, my Saviour.
For He has looked with favour on the
lowliness of His servant.
Surely, from now on all generations will call
me blessed;
for the Mighty One has done great things for
me, and holy is His name.
His mercy is for those who fear Him from
generation to generation.
He has shown strength with His arm;
He has scattered the proud in the thoughts
of their hearts.
He has brought down the powerful from
their thrones, and lifted up the lowly;
He has filled the hungry with good things,
and sent the rich away empty.
He has helped His servant Israel, in
remembrance of His mercy, according to the
promise He made to our ancestors, to
Abraham and to his descendants for ever.'*

Luke 1: 46-55

S·PETER   S·MARY   S·IOHN   S·IAMES

To the memory of MARY ANN eldest daughter ...   ...tenant General READ of Crowood and ... in which sleep in Jesus ...   wife of IOHN RICHMOND SEYMOUR Esq will God bring with him ...   This window is erected by her six children 1861

The stained glass window

Representations in the four large lights are of St Peter with the keys to the heavenly Kingdom, the Virgin Mary holding a lily symbolising love and beauty, St John the Evangelist holding a chalice with a swan in it, and St James with his letter in the Scriptures. Fruits and leaves of the vine appear in the glass above.

The stained glass was inserted in 1861 in memory of Mary Ann, daughter of Lt Gen. Read of Crowood, and wife of John Richmond Seymour. Crowood is a house and estate to the north-east of the village.

The rebuilding of the Chapel in 1891: The whole of the south and east walls of this aisle were demolished in 1891 as they were so unsafe. They were rebuilt using much of the original materials. All the ashlar limestone was replaced round the windows in the exact positions as before. This is confirmed by remnants of the medieval wall paintings on these stones, which follow on from one to another. Thus this chapel was reconstructed as when it was built in the late fourteenth century, though without the steps up to the rood loft. The wooden roof, as in the north aisle, was newly built in 1891.

The Anglo-Saxon stones had been found in the south-east angle of the east wall of the nave, and lying just below ground level by the footings of this wall. One reason why the north and south aisles had to be rebuilt was because they had no foundations and after years of burials, both inside and outside the church, the walls were seriously undermined.

The Bishop of Salisbury's angels: The present Bishop of Salisbury, the Right Reverend Dr David Stancliffe, has kindly passed on the following delightful story, continuing the special link between Salisbury and Ramsbury.

'When I first came to Ramsbury after becoming Bishop [in 1993] I was struck by the carved angels on the side [of the litany desk], and realised that I had seen them before. Puzzling over this, I mentioned it to my mother, who said that when my father had briefly been curate in Ramsbury, and we had lodged in the Old Rectory, I had often been in the church, and I had always been fascinated by that carving. The next time I came to Ramsbury I sat on the floor, to get a child's eye view of the carving, and suddenly realised that they have stayed in my mind all those years. I cannot have been more than two, as we were only nine months in Ramsbury and then left to go to Cirencester. I think, therefore that it must have been my earliest memory of a distinct place.'

Now walk down the south aisle to the fellowship area. →

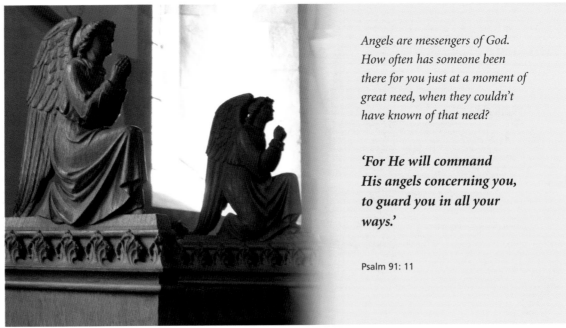

Angels are messengers of God. How often has someone been there for you just at a moment of great need, when they couldn't have known of that need?

'For He will command His angels concerning you, to guard you in all your ways.'

Psalm 91: 11

THE SOUTH AISLE and FELLOWSHIP AREA [12]

The memorials on the walls, professionally cleaned in 2003, are mainly to members of the Read and Seymour families of Crowood.

One, the work of a noted Flemish sculptor P.M. van der Gelder, is in the style which was prevalent in England at the end of the eighteenth century. It is a beautiful memorial of a draped female figure, grieving over an urn which has on its base a shield charged with the armorial bearings of the deceased, Henry Read, and his wife.

An unworked Purbeck 'marble' stone on the floor may possibly have been an early altar stone, with its face turned downwards.

By the south door is another holy water stoup. Beyond the door, on the wall, is the Millennium Tapestry. The brainchild of Canon David Howe, it was worked by a team of local embroiderers led by Canon Howe, Jane Handford and Liz McIndoe. The original drawings of parts of the village were by Eric Kilner.

The clock in the south-west corner was installed in the church in 1866. The cost of £136 was raised by public subscription. Abandoned in the tower when an electric unit replaced it in 1966, it was rescued and reconditioned by Ronny Price in 1977.

On the stone pier of the tower, to the right of the door to the ringing chamber and tower, can be seen the carved initials IW. These may refer to the Revd John Wilde, Vicar of Ramsbury from 1599-1663.

If you have not already done so, and before you leave the church, you may like to pause in the stillness and peace of God.

'PEACE'

'Sweet Peace, where dost thou dwell?
I humbly crave,
Let me once know.
I sought thee in a secret cave,
And ask'd, if Peace were there.
A hollow winde did seem to answer, No:
Go seek elsewhere.

I did; and going did a rainbow note:
Surely, thought I,
This is the lace of Peaces coat:
I will search the matter.
But while I lookt, the clouds immediately
Did break and scatter.

Then went I to a garden, and did spy
A gallant flower,
The Crown Imperiall: Sure, said I,
Peace at the root must dwell.
But when I digg'd, I saw a worm devoure
What show'd so well.

At length I met a rev'rend good old man,
Whom when for Peace
I did demand, he thus began:
There was a Prince of old
At Salem dwelt, who liv'd with
good increase
Of flock and fold.

He sweetly liv'd; yet sweetnesse
did not save
His life from foes.
But after death out of his grave
There sprang twelve stalks of wheat:
Which many wondring at, got some
of those
To plant and set.

It prosper'd strangely, and did
soon disperse
Through all the earth:
For they that taste it do rehearse,
That vertue lies therein,
A secret vertue bringing peace and mirth
By flight of sinne.

Take of this grain, which in my
garden grows,
And grows for you;
Make bread of it: and that repose
And peace, which ev'ry where
With so much earnestnesse you do pursue,
Is onely there.'

George Herbert (1593-1633)

Now move to the south door. →

THE SOUTH DOOR AND PORCH [13]

Until the seventeenth century churches were places of sanctuary, thus the doors and ironwork were heavy to withstand invaders. The wooden doors with iron fixtures, are possibly fifteenth century, set in what is thought to be a thirteenth century doorway. It might have been moved from the part of the medieval church which was first built.

'I am the door: by Me if any man enter in he shall be saved.'

Revelations 3: 20

God cannot be imprisoned in holy places; we cannot capture His transcendence. God is all around us, everywhere, in everything, but He is also within each one of us. So as we leave the church we walk with Him out into His world, in love and peace, through the power of His Holy Spirit, to serve Him.

'God is love, and those who abide in love abide in God, and God abides in them.'

1 John 4:16

'No one has ever seen God; if we love one another, God lives in us, and His love is perfected in us.'

1 John 4:12

The porch

Given in 1891, at a cost of £400, by the vicar, the Revd Harry Baber, in memory of his wife, the present porch replaces an earlier 'mean erection' of the late eighteenth century.

The four stained glass windows represent women of the Old Testament: Sarah, with a plate of cakes, Hannah, with her son Samuel, Rachel with a jar of water, and Ruth with sheaves of corn. The roof is of oak. On either side are benches where women used to leave their pattens (overshoes) before entering the church.

In the niche above the entrance is a carved stone Virgin and Child, with the words below: 'Unto us a child is born, unto us a Son is given.' In the spandrels on either side of the arch are, on the left, the coat of arms of the see of Canterbury, and on the right the arms of the Baber family. Sadly, Harry Baber died before the porch was completed.

Porches: By the fourteenth century, porches on churches had become necessities. They were of particular importance in the medieval period. Usually they were built on the sunnier, favoured south side, as at Holy Cross, unless the manor house was to the north of the church. The north door used to be called the 'devil's door'.

Many community activities and much secular business, as well as religious rituals, took place in the porch. For example, marriage banns were called, penitents received absolution, women knelt to be 'churched' after the birth of a child, couples were asked if they consented to marriage before going inside to a Nuptial Mass, coroners' courts were held, civil business took place, and public notices displayed.

A room above was often used as a school and this may have been the case in Ramsbury in 1475 when the Wootton and York chantry provided 'poor and indigent' scholars with the 'rudiments of grammar', or in 1660 when the curate, Henry Dent, was expected to teach local children as part of his job.

As you leave this place of prayer and time of stillness, and return to the busy world, you may like to consider the words of St Teresa of Avila (1515-82):

'**Christ has no body now on earth but yours, no hands but yours, no feet but yours.**

Yours are the eyes through which must look out Christ's compassion on the world.

Yours are the feet with which He is to go about doing good.

Yours are the hands with which He is to bless men now.'

THE CHURCHYARD AND LYCHGATE [14]

A leaflet on the churchyard and tombs, compiled by Ronny Price, is available in the church.

The churchyard may have originated as a pre-Christian burial ground. With the spread of Christianity a cross, or possibly two for Ramsbury (see Saxon stones, pages 6-7), would have been erected as a central memorial for all the dead buried in it. The crosses may have pre-dated the building of the Saxon cathedral minster.

Notice that the graves tend to face east with the feet towards the rising sun, as a sign of hope. The table tombstones near the south door may have been used for distributing loaves of bread to the poor. Most of the gravestones date from the seventeenth century, as before then people were buried in the church itself. That practice ceased, partly because of the smell and partly because space ran out, despite burying on top of previous graves. Internal burial was finally forbidden by an Act of Parliament in 1854.

The eastern part of the churchyard is kept as an area for wildlife, under the Wiltshire Living Churchyard and Cemetery Project. It was given the Bishop's Award 2003 for Continued Good Management for Wildlife, in association with the Wiltshire Wildlife Trust.

The churchyard as the centre of medieval village life: The churchyard was the centre of village life. Travelling merchants would set up their stalls and booths, and the fairs, held on 3 May and 15 September in honour of the Holy Cross, took place there. Games were played including fives between the tower buttresses, while tug-o'-war, bowling, and dancing followed the annual event of church ales, and dancing round the Maypoles on May Day brought fun to the daily round.

The Lychgate

Lych is from the Old English word 'lic' meaning dead body or corpse. The Lychgate was built as a place of shelter for coffins and pallbearers before coming into church for the funeral service. The priest met the coffin to be given the legal burial certificate outside the church. Now the priest may meet the coffin there, as a mark of respect.

The present Lychgate was built in 1910 in memory of James Lovegrove Waldron and John Waldron of Marridge Hill. They, with others in the family, set up a sheep-farming venture in the Falkland Islands and Patagonia, in South America, as employment for impoverished Ramsbury labourers at the end of the nineteenth century. There are still family connections in the village with people who went out there. Some returned but others stayed.

Having spent time inside the church you may like to look further at some of the outside features of the building.

Notice:

- the use of local flints, which before 1891 were covered in plaster like the chancel and painted a 'vulgar' yellow,

- the gargoyles used as rainwater spouts to throw water clear of the walls, but now decorative as drainpipes take the water away,

- the line of the drip-mould of the medieval steep-pitched roof on the tower,

- the sundial on the south wall,

- the thirteenth-century west door and niche above it,

- the fine thirteenth-century traceried west window.

Gargoyles: the word comes from the Latin 'gurgulio' meaning throat. They were used to throw water clear of the church. Without gargoyles water from the roofs would have poured down to the base of the walls and undermined the footings, especially at Ramsbury where the north and south walls had no proper foundations.

The gargoyles were thought to scare away the devil and local carvers, probably with much delight, made the expressions as frightening as possible, and rarely holy.

Although drainage pipes were introduced, gargoyles were still used.

Sundials: Most churches in medieval times were coated in a form of cement which was limewashed, both inside and out. Mass dials were painted on the walls and a metal rod, or gnomon, was attached to cast a shadow.

In the eighteenth century, sundials were commonly placed on churches for the local people to tell the time, as on the outside of the south aisle wall of Holy Cross.

EPILOGUE

In our journey round Holy Cross, we may have discovered not only historical and architectural detail, but also spiritual thoughts and insights on the nature and meaning of the living God, in whose praise this church was built.

It is God who is the still centre of our being. He makes Himself known in the silence and it is to Him that we need to turn, to counteract the desires and forces in our lives which tend to pull us apart.

He reveals to us our real selves, and challenges us, making our hearts restless for His presence, encouraging us to seek Him in the silence in which the glorious answer is experienced.

'Drop thy still dews of quietness,
till all our strivings cease;
take from our souls the strain and stress,
and let our ordered lives confess the beauty of Thy peace.

Breathe through the heats of our desire
Thy coolness and Thy balm;
let sense be dumb, let flesh retire;
speak through the earthquake, wind, and fire,
O still small voice of calm!'

J.G.Whittier (1807-82)

✠ *'The Lord bless you and keep you;*
The Lord make His face to shine upon you,
and be gracious to you;
The Lord turn His face towards you,
and give you peace.'

Numbers 6: 24-26

APPENDIX 1: Further points of interest

The Reformation and its effects on the villagers

Churches from the seventh to the sixteenth centuries were primarily shelters for altars. People attended church to see and hear the priests celebrate the Roman Catholic Latin Mass. They knew the rhythm of it even if they couldn't read or understand the Latin.

The Reformation, sparked off by Henry VIII's need for a male heir, must have caused total confusion to the clergy and villagers. Although Henry broke with the Roman Catholics in the 1534 Act of Supremacy, which abolished the Pope's power in England, and became Head of the Church of England, the services still closely followed the Mass, but with his son, Edward VI's, accession the Prayer Book was introduced. On Whitsunday 1549, Holy Communion was first celebrated in English.

The order went out to strip the churches of all their relics, statues, screens, paintings, stained glass and ornaments, as well as vestments and communion plate. The many ancient and popular rituals, festivals and observances were prohibited, bringing a huge change to community life, including the loss of much fun and entertainment. The churchwardens had to destroy or sell everything connected with the Catholic faith while the clergy were expected to change to Protestant liturgy and grapple with the idea of being able to marry.

Just four years later Edward died and his sister, Mary, became Queen and every church was told to buy or reinstate all that had been sold or destroyed. The expense for the churches was great, and what happened to the clergy wives?

No sooner had this been done, than within five years Mary had died and Elizabeth came to the throne, so all Catholic images had to go once again. There is no record of the feelings of the people or clergy, except that, through fear, they very speedily obeyed. Certainly their security in and intense attachment to the parish church would have been shaken. A few local families, such as the Gillmores at Elm Down, on Springs Hill, and the Waldrons of Marridge Hill, secretly maintained their Catholic faith, and some were charged with recusancy.

The effects of the Reformation were many:

- The role of the church in community life was greatly diminished, as there were no more mystery plays, pilgrimages, religious processions, parish revels, play acting, pageants or church ales.
- Long sermons were introduced into services, together with pulpits and pews.

- The inside of the church was stripped bare, the walls whitewashed and texts painted on, in particular the Lord's Prayer, the Creed and the Ten Commandments.
- The chantries, including the Wootton and York chantry in Holy Cross, were dissolved by 1547 so no more money was paid for Masses to be said for the souls of the departed.
- Endowments for lamps in the church, as from Lamplands across the River Kennet, or for the care of the sick and elderly, or for education, all ceased.
- The clergy and churchwardens were loaded with many duties of the parish, including the care of the poor, the collection of church rates, the upkeep of highways and bridges, as well as the maintenance of the church.

Despite this, the people didn't lose their devotion to the church. The Act of Uniformity in 1559 ordered that everyone should attend their parish church at least once on a Sunday. This was enforced by the church courts, although there were many and varied excuses. Thus the Sunday services were still the only occasions when the whole parish, men and women alike, met together. They became gatherings of great importance in the social life of the village.

Church services

The three services each Sunday before the Reformation were Matins, Mass, and Evensong in the afternoon. Everyone had to attend Mass on Sunday and on as many other Holy days as they could. The three services were replaced, after the Reformation, by Morning and Evening Prayer, with occasional Holy Communion. This had to be celebrated at least four times a year.

With no heating, the church was very cold in winter. The heat in summer was made worse by the smell from the bodies buried under the beaten earth floor, or in the vaults. Compulsory attendance meant parishioners crowded onto the benches, encouraging shuffling, talking, bad behaviour and quarrelling, according to the church court records. The performance of public penance during a service was also a common sentence given by the courts.

Some relaxation on attendance set in with James I and Charles I, who both encouraged Sunday sports, which were accompanied by much drunken revelry.

Morning and Evening Prayer and Holy Communion continued through the centuries, with some liturgical changes. In the 1864 Archdeacon's Visitation to Holy

Cross, when JCCBP Hawkins was vicar and Jacob Sturton curate, there was Morning Prayer at 11.0 am, with a sermon, Evening Prayer at 3.0 pm, twice monthly with baptism, and Evensong at 6.0 pm, again with a sermon. Holy Communion was on the first Sunday in each month, also at Christmas, on Easter Day and Good Friday. There were 110 communicants at Festivals and 60 on other occasions. That year there were 93 baptisms, 12 couples were married, and 53 burials. Accounts of the collections were kept but not made public![12]

Over the last twenty-five years the Communion service has assumed more importance as the main Sunday service in Holy Cross, with additional family services to encourage children and young families.

The Civil War and Commonwealth

The Civil War brought strict non-conformist Puritanism and further destruction in the churches, with any remaining stained glass smashed, statues, vestments, organs, service books and carved woodwork destroyed, usually by out-of-control troops. Holy Cross was visited in 1643 by a Colonel Symonds, of the King's Troop, who noted that the brasses had already been stolen from tombs, possibly by one or other of the armies.

The altar was moved to the centre of the chancel at this time, with chairs round it.

The vicar, John Wilde, though noted for his Puritanism, was removed from the living of Ramsbury by 1646, but he was reinstated in 1660.

The restoration of the monarchy

With Charles II's restoration in 1660, the Anglican church was re-established. In 1662 The Book of Common Prayer was revived and music returned, with the singing of Psalms. The altar was moved to the east end of the church and railed. Gifts were made to the church, to help offset the desecration of the Reformation and Civil War, such as the communion plate and altar cloths. In 1751 the two fine chandeliers were given.

The clergy

The vicars were often 'unlearned but dedicated men, of simple piety and deep pastoral care.' With the complex pre-Reformation Latin liturgy and numerous festivals, a number of clergy were on hand to help the vicar with services. Even with fewer, and simpler, services after the Reformation, by 1730 Holy Cross still had one, or sometimes two, curates.

Occasionally the vicars ended up in court for various failings but the majority were honest men, struggling to care for their parishioners on a pitifully low stipend, unless they had independent means, as with the Meyricks in the early nineteenth century (page 29).

The vicar's income at Ramsbury, despite being augmented by the state, was low, even though the parish was large. No record of a complaint by a vicar has been found though.

In 1756 the vicar, Richard Garrard (1737-86) received the following annual income:

	£	s	d
Tyths [sic]	28.	15.	0
Hay, corn, grass	36.	7.	6
Wood	7.	6.	3
Churchings	3.	10.	6
Marriages	8.	3.	0
Burials	9.	1.	2
Offertories and in Easter book	22.	6.	6
Total	£115.	9.	11[13]

In 1783 it had increased to £160.3s.6d including rent from land in Swan's Bottom and the Marshes, along the Kennet river. The value of hay and corn had increased considerably, to £84.15s.0d. In return for their glebeland the vicars were also expected to supply a bull and boar for parish use.

As farming improved in the eighteenth century, bringing increased tithes, the clergy became wealthier so many large Georgian rectories and vicarages were built. However, in Ramsbury, Richard Garrard let the vicarage get into disrepair, so it was replaced with a new house, on the same site, in about 1810 (the present Old Vicarage).

Some clergy became JPs and seemed more like the country squire than a vicar, such as Edward Graves Meyrick. Many clergy were non-resident and left the work of the parish and services to their wives or to curates.

Eighteenth-century clergy often seemed more concerned with keeping the status quo of social class order than with any spiritual growth or welfare of their parishioners. Jane Austen depicts this well in the character of Mr Collins in her novel *Pride and Prejudice*.

In 1840, the Revd JCCBP Hawkins was licensed to Holy Cross and was noted as 'a wondrous type of old-fashioned parson – a true gentleman, an honest man and everything except a theologian!' Another opinion was that he was 'strong-voiced, muscular, outspoken, dictatorial, magisterial-minded and a mannered autocrat.' Whatever the view of him, the church was full each week.

As a contrast, later that century, the Revd Harry Baber (1872-92) became vicar *(below)*. He was said to be a 'gentle-spoken, dignified, courteous, amiable parish priest with a strong sense of the Vicariate that was his.' His special gift was 'taking advantage of the assistance offered him by ladies, whom he had the especial power of keeping under control and with all this a most graceful and consummate tact.'[14]

Non-conformity

In response to the general attitude of the clergy in the seventeenth and eighteenth centuries, dissension grew in protest at the Anglican church. In Ramsbury, Henry Dent, a Fellow of Wadham College, Oxford from 1656-9, became curate at Holy Cross in 1660 to the vicar, John Wilde. His non-conformist views caused great friction and he was excommunicated three times but bought his absolution each time.

In 1663 John Wilde died and John Wilson took over as vicar. Wilson became Dent's most bitter enemy and persecuted him without mercy. Dent preached in the fields and woods surrounding Ramsbury and beyond. He resigned as curate and many villagers, dissatisfied with the care given to them by the vicar, followed him in setting up the Presbyterian faith in the village. From this

followed Methodism and Congregationalism as a strong force in Ramsbury through the ensuing centuries. Meetings of Quakers and Mormons also began, with some emigrating to America in the seventeenth to nineteenth centuries.

Church plate

With the restoration of the monarchy and the re-establishment of the Anglican communion, there was a need for church plate. Before the Reformation, in 1405, there had been a silver and gilt chalice (for the wine), with a crucifixion on it, and two other silver and gilt chalices with patens (plates for the wafers).

In 1685 Samuel Jones, of the Manor, gave a silver salver and new communion table, with a damask cloth and two napkins. His son, Richard Jones, was also generous. Although only one silver paten, hallmarked 1719, was known to have been donated by him, it is possible a flagon, hallmarked 1707, and a silver chalice and another paten, dated 1719, were also given by him. A copy of the 1719 chalice was given in 1839 by the vicar at that time, the Revd J.W.Dundas. An apostle spoon, of St Matthew, dated 1661, was given by Mrs Freeman, of the village in 1881, and the Revd Harry Baber, vicar during the 1891 restoration, donated a brass alms dish at Easter 1889. The Ashley family gave an ornate chalice and a ciborium with cover for the wafers, to commemorate their residence in the village from 1700 to 1958.

Notes from the Registers

Parish registers first had to be kept, along with Churchwardens' accounts, wills and doctrinal books, in 1567. However, the earliest registers which still exist for Holy Cross are dated 1678. Chests had to be provided, by the

churchwardens, in which to keep the registers, vestments, Bibles and Peter's Pence, the church's contribution to the Pope. Three old chests survive in Holy Cross for these purposes.

Apart from the records of baptisms, marriages and burials, the registers include a few additional notes.

OCT 15TH 1680

Elizabeth Wilson, widow of the vicar, John Wilson [1663-1680], had bought various items in the vicarage from Mrs Wilde, widow of Wilson's predecessor, John Wilde [1599-1663]. Elizabeth in turn sold items to Benjamin Malden 'in the summe of forty shillings'. They included:

The Wainscott in ye Parlour
The Settles and the Wainscott in the Hall
The Hedges next the Churchyard
and other items

JULY 14TH 1681

'An account of money given by parishioners towards repairs for the vicarage house, totalling £45.17s.5d.

Sir Seymour Pile Baronett	2.	00.	00
Francis Pile Esq	1.	00.	00
Lady Elizabeth Pile	1.	00.	00
Robert Gilmore Esq	1.	00.	00
Thomas Hill	0.	5.	00
Widow George	0.	2.	6
Thomas Jennings	0.	5.	00
Etc'			

1685

'Memorandum that in the year 1685 I, Thomas Hawes Vicar of Ramsbury did give to the Widdow Horne the Lopp of the Ashes growing on the south side of the Church, which she desired because her husband planted them, upon Mr Wilds promise, the then incumbent, yt they should have the advantage of the first Lopp, they for the future being to make no pretence thereunto, but the said trees and ye lopp or other benefits accrewing thereby, to remain to the Vicar of Ramsbury and his successors notwithstanding.

Witness my hand
Thomas Hawes [1685-1717]'

It was Thomas Hawes who received various items of silver and a communion table from Samuel Jones of the Manor.

1686

'An account of ye names of such persons who have had certificates in order to avouch for ye cure of the disease called ye Kingsevill since my induction to ye Vicarage of Ramsbury:

Sarah Appleford	Aug 22 1686
Joan Hewbury	Aug 22 1686
Anne Lay & Catharine Bayman	Aug 25 1686
Ursula Watts & Elizabeth Pearse	Aug 25 1686
Elizabeth Pithouse	Aug 27 1686
Rebecca Kingstone	Aug 27 1686
Mary Long	Feb 27 1686
Grace ye daughter of Ed. Knackstone	Mar 13 1686
Frances ye daughter of Thomas Allowe	Ap 17 1688'

It was believed that the Sovereign, from Edward the Confessor on, could cure the King's Evil, or scrofula (a disease with glandular swellings and tendency to consumption, leading to death) by touch. The practice, undertaken at particular times of the year, ceased in George 1's reign. Bath Abbey church was probably the closest place for Ramsbury people to go, when the Sovereign visited there. Notice it was only women who seemed to suffer this disease, and from the well-off families as well as poorer ones. For instance, the Knackstones, Applefords and Baymans were all farmers or in thriving trades in the village.

A number of women were whipped and given passes to move out of the parish:

1694 May 26	Mary the wife of George Mason w'l five small children to Dover in Kent.
1698 March 15	Susanna Athead to Westbury under the plain in Wilts.
1699 April 1	Anne Herring to St James, Westminster.

Most people had to have been born in their parishes to receive the poor rate. If they came from another parish and fell on hard times they were sent back to their original home parishes rather than be a burden on the ratepayers of Ramsbury.

The burials registers record a number of people buried in wool following the Parliamentary Act for Burying in Woollen in 1666. This Act was to boost the woollen industry. The first affirmation (affidavit) that this had occurred was signed by Seymour Pile, of Crowood, at the burial of Thomas Whiteyate senr., on 24 October

1678. It had to be made in front of a JP and two credible witnesses.

Another note states that 'Alexander the sonne of Alexander Porter was buried the tenth day of October…[and] was not put in, wrapt or wound up, or buried in any shirt, shift or shroud, made or mingled with Flax, Hemp, Silk, Hair, Gold or Silver or othr than what is made of sheeps wool onely, nor in any coffin lined or faced with any cloth, stuff, or any other thing whatsoever made or mingled with Flax, Hemp, Silk, Hair, Gold or Silver, or any other material but sheeps Wool onely….16 October 1678.'

Samuel Jones, of the Manor, however, was buried in linen in 1686 and his estate had to pay a £5 fine.

Finally, a note about the allocation of pews in Holy Cross.
'These are to Certifie that in the year of our Lord God 1682 Mary the wife of Robert Mabberley was placed in the fourth place of the widow Hills of Preston, the widow Hill by her daughter, and widow Webbe sitting above her – By us

Robert Mabberley
Edward Jones   Churchwardens.'

Building materials and repairs

As with any building, over the centuries repairs have had to be made to the structure of Holy Cross. Fortunately, the main body of the church was made of flints which are some of the strongest materials to use as they neither change nor weather. With so many in the fields around the village it is unlikely they were brought from elsewhere.

However, the quoins (corner or edging stones) are of ashlar, which is dressed stone, in this case limestone. This must have been brought in the thirteenth century either from the Bath area or from Purbeck, in Dorset, by wagon and horses, or more likely oxen, due to the weight of the stone. The so-called Purbeck marble, which is used in Holy Cross for tombs and the piscina on the right in the sanctuary, is not marble but limestone which can be highly polished.

Any material from the old Anglo-Saxon cathedral was also used, as well as the Anglo-Saxon crosses and memorial slabs, all of Bath stone, which were incorporated in the south wall of the nave and south aisle. Portions of two thirteenth-century memorials were cut and used as window arches by the fourteenth-century builders, and some stones of Norman workmanship were also used.

In medieval times a form of cement was used to coat the inside and outside walls and this was then given a limewash. In about 1807 the antiquarian, Sir Richard Colt Hoare, recorded that 'the venerable old stone turret of the church has just undergone a complete yellow-washing and in the eyes of its vulgar inhabitants is much beautified and improved. If conspicuousness is desirable, this end is most completely obtained for no object in the whole vale is so much so.'[15] In 1842 the church was repainted inside and out.

The original steep-pitched nave roof was replaced in the early sixteenth century by a lower pitch, lead-covered one. At the same time the walls of the nave were raised and clerestory windows inserted. These helped to bring more light into the nave, which had become much darker when the north and south aisles were built at the end of the fourteenth century. They also threw more light onto the internal roof, so the fine new oak tie-beam rafters could be better appreciated.

New, larger, windows were put in the chancel and the east window of the south aisle in the fifteenth century, replacing smaller openings. They are similar to those put in the Darrell chapel when it was built at that time.

Windows: Anglo-Saxon churches usually had small, slit windows which were high up in the walls to try to stop draughts. The first windows would either have had shutters or covers of oiled canvas, or possibly nothing at all, to stop the wind, rain and cold from getting in. Churchgoers were hardy souls then!

The Normans introduced stained glass into churches but the general use of glass for windows came in the thirteenth century, a major time for church building. As the technical skills developed it was possible to make larger windows, as in Holy Cross, in the fourteenth and fifteenth centuries.

Although there was a wealth of stained glass in medieval churches, much of it was destroyed during the Reformation and Civil War. The majority of stained glass in churches dates from the 1840s to 1870s. The Holy Cross stained glass dates from the 1870s to 1907.

During Richard Garrard's fifty-year tenure as vicar the fabric of the church was largely neglected, so that by 1780 it needed urgent repairs on the roof and galleries.

In 1836 the following payments were made for various repairs:

By Luker for Deals and labour, repair of church	£42.	13s.	2d
By Luker as above for lead and labour relaying the gutters, casting old lead and relaying a part of the roof	£68.	1s.	8d
By Martin plaster and slating	£17.	2s.	4$\frac{1}{2}$d
By Blackwell for Lime	£2.	10s.	3d
By W. Edwards carriage of Lime and Sand	£1.	15s.	0d
By G. Sims for cask of cement	£1.	1s.	0d
By Luker repair of windows		18s.	0d

In 1838 new gates to the churchyard (£10), iron gates for the porch (£8.19s.0d), new bellropes, stone for the windows, repairing the belfry windows, a pulpit mat, lamps and candles all had to be paid for. Over £300 was spent in 1854 on the tower alone due to its rotten state:

Iron	£23.	14s.	3d
Timber and work	£95.	12s.	7d
Lead and work	£137.	12s.	11d
Men	£1.	14s.	11d
Beer	£2.	4s.	4d.

Notice the beer cost more than the labour!

A further £18 was spent on repairs by Baroness Angela Burdett-Coutts following a survey she had done in 1879. Ten years later the church was in some danger of collapse. Emergency shoring up of the south aisle wall was necessary while a full survey was made for the extensive restoration of 1891-2. The architect was Doran Webb.

Over one hundred years later, in 1998, another programme of work was begun, this time on the lead roof, windows, stonework and interior, as well as a new heating system and complete rewiring and new lighting.

The 1891-2 restoration

The original church walls had been built without solid foundations, only their great thickness had kept them standing. The soil was bad for building and constant

burials also undermined their stability. Both the north and south aisle walls had to be demolished and reconstructed, leading to the discovery of the Anglo-Saxon stones. With the internal and external cement stucco removed it was obvious the mortar had disintegrated. The paintings inside, which had survived the Reformation, were in too bad a state to preserve.

Many roof timbers were completely worm eaten to 'no more than a shell of fibre filled in with dust,' and had to be

replaced. It was decided not to return the roof to the pre-fifteenth century steep pitch.

The whole floor of the church was taken up and relaid with concrete, then asphalt and finally the stone paving and wood block flooring. The asphalt and removal of earth from the external side walls helped to make the church drier. Sadly no excavation was undertaken while the floor was up to try to find the foundations of the Anglo-Saxon cathedral.

Despite the repairs thirty years earlier, the tower was in a very bad state. The external stucco was carefully removed, revealing the flint facing which had become completely loose. All the flints were removed in sections, the cracks cut out, bonding stones inserted to bolster weak points, and the flints replaced with strong cement. All agreed the tower was greatly improved without the stucco.

Inside the church the galleries were removed, the organ moved to its present position, thus opening up the tower arch and letting light flood into the nave through the traceried thirteenth-century west window *(above right)*. The box pews were thrown out as they were thought to make the church very dark and gloomy. They were replaced by chairs until the present pews were put in a few years later, in 1903.

A new boiler was installed in the heating chamber under the organ. It lasted until 1946 when another was put in. This lasted until 1998 when the whole heating system was renewed and overhauled.

The chancel was restored by Sir Francis Burdett, 7th Baronet, at his sole expense. The internal plaster was removed revealing the arcade of arches, doorway and other stonework within the walls. The lower part of the east window was exposed, having been covered by erections behind the altar. However, the Georgian ceiling was left, even though it truncates the top of the window. The old timbers of the original roof can be seen through a small pierced opening on the outside, above the east window. A small porch was added to the priest's door on the south side.

The font was moved to its present position in front of the vestry. The pulpit was erected in memory of the vicar, the Revd Harry Baber, who had paid for the porch to be built in memory of his wife.

Numerous gifts were given to complete the furnishing of Holy Cross; the oak, which was limed in the 1960s, being particularly attractive.[16] Pevsner records that Holy Cross has 'quite an uncommon wealth' of furnishings.

Fund-raising

Who paid for the church to be built, being such a vast building compared to the villagers huts? How was its upkeep paid for through the centuries? Not only the building, but the clergy fees and costs of worship needed to be found.

The presence of the important Anglo-Saxon iron-smelting forge of the seventh to eighth centuries suggested wealth in the village. The establishment of the bishopric and the high value of the Hundred of Ramsbury in the Domesday record, confirms the prosperity. Thus the Anglo-Saxon cathedral minster would have reflected this wealth and was, for the time, probably a large and architecturally elaborate building.

Although Herman, the tenth Bishop of Ramsbury, complained of the poverty of the ecclesiastical establishment, the Bishops of Salisbury, with their 'palace' in the park to the west of the village, accrued enough wealth to rebuild the church. As the population increased after the ravages of the Black Death in 1349, and the Bishops used it for ordinations, it was enlarged to the fine proportions we see today, and greatly decorated and furnished.

By the time of the Reformation, the church nationally owned a quarter of the wealth of the whole country. In addition local people endowed chantries, as with the Wootton and York chantry in Holy Cross, and money was given to say Mass for the souls of the dead, or to provide education or food for the poor.

At the heart of the village, the church building and worship were central in the villagers' lives and its maintenance and upkeep was of great importance to them. It is to their credit that they gave so generously. They were expected to give Mass pennies at each service of Mass, light scot (tax) for the candles, payment for burial, and Peter's pence, which was for the Pope. If anyone missed a service they were fined and, of course, a tenth, or tithe, of all they produced had to be given to the prebend and vicar. The prebend received the greater tithes of corn and hay, and the vicar the lesser tithes of milk, cheese and vegetables. However, we have seen that the Ramsbury vicarage was a poor one so the vicar was given the prebend's corn tithes as well. The tithes were commuted to money payments by the 1841 tithe award for Ramsbury.

Henry VIII's need to control the power and influence of the church brought the dissolution of the monasteries and the Reformation. In 1553 the King took 3oz of silver plate from Holy Cross, leaving a chalice of 11oz. Anything of value in the church was sold or hidden, but the various taxes and tithes continued. The Peter's pence possibly went to the Bishops instead of the Pope.

The main event to raise money for the upkeep of the church was known as 'church ales', held in the churchyard. Each year the churchwardens asked farmers to contribute malt from their barley for the ale wives to brew strong ale, at Church House by the lychgate in Ramsbury. Other produce was donated to make vegetable stews, spit roasts and fresh bread for a village feast. All the parishioners paid their dues and ate and drank their fill. Afterwards there was general merrymaking with 'dancing, bowling, and shooting at buttes', as the 'ancients sat gravely by looking on.' A good sum of money was raised for the church. It was a rowdy occasion and not to be compared with our church fetes of today! The Puritans frowned on it and the custom finally died out in the eighteenth century.

Although fines from the church courts would have been another source of income, eventually it became necessary to introduce a church rate, levied on all in the parish, to pay not only for the church but also, from the sixteenth century, for the relief of the poor, and maintenance of the highways and bridges as well. In the eighteenth century additional income came from the rents from the box pews in the church.

In 1834, the first year of the only existing churchwardens' accounts for Holy Cross, the church rate was set at 1/2d in the pound, but in 1835 it was increased to 3d in the pound and the following year to 6d in the pound to pay for extensive repairs to the church.

A further small source of extra revenue came from the fine levied by the churchwardens for drunkenness in the village. For example, in 1838 a shilling was paid by each of twelve offenders, two of whom were women.[17]

Through the centuries, villagers have given generously to Holy Cross, but a much greater effort was needed to pay for the 1891 restoration, and the most recent work since 1998. Fund-raising provided entertainment for all. The Grand Bazaar on 16 and 17 July 1891 at the Manor was a great success. Stalls, run by Lady Burdett and other ladies from the village, were prettily draped and arranged with numerous fancy goods. The refreshment tent was constantly busy, providing 'luscious fruit and iced drinks' and meals of hams, chickens, and eggs, supplied by the local farmers, with tea using water boiled up by Stephen Osmond, using his steam engine.

There was boating on the lake, a performance by the Ramsbury Mummers and music by the Swindon Town Military Band.

A similar event at Littlecote House in 1894 helped to raise the final £500 towards the £6000 needed, although the church had been re-opened the year before. On Tuesday, 8 August 1893, at 3.0 pm, led by the Baroness Burdett-Coutts and Lady Burdett, the congregation filled every corner as the Bishop of Salisbury and the Archdeacon of Wiltshire entered the church for the re-opening service. Tea afterwards was provided at Parliament Piece by the Batson family, before the Bishop attended Evensong and delivered the sermon.

An appeal for £120,000 was launched in 1998 for repairs to the lead roof, full rewiring, a new heating system and work on the windows and stonework. The generosity of many benefactors, both locally and further distant, made it possible to reach the target. A Grand Bazaar in the Memorial Hall, Holy Cross and the Church Room raised £6000, while a similar amount was given from the proceeds of two concerts organised by Music in Country Churches, on the 9 and 10 July 1999. The first was given by the Belcea String Quartet and the second by the pianist, Maria João Pires in the presence of the Prince of Wales, Patron of Music in Country Churches.

The end of the tithes, pew rents and the church rate when the local councils and their rating system were introduced, deprived the church of its income. There is constant financial concern on how to maintain this Grade 1 listed building and surrounding churchyard walls, cover the costs of services for the community, the upkeep of the churchyard, and the ever increasing parish share, at present £32,593 a year, which goes to the Diocese to pay, among other things, for clergy and their pensions. Apart from a grant towards the churchyard maintenance from the Parish Council, the income comes entirely from the support of the Church members and community.

APPENDIX 2: Architect's drawings of Holy Cross in 1890

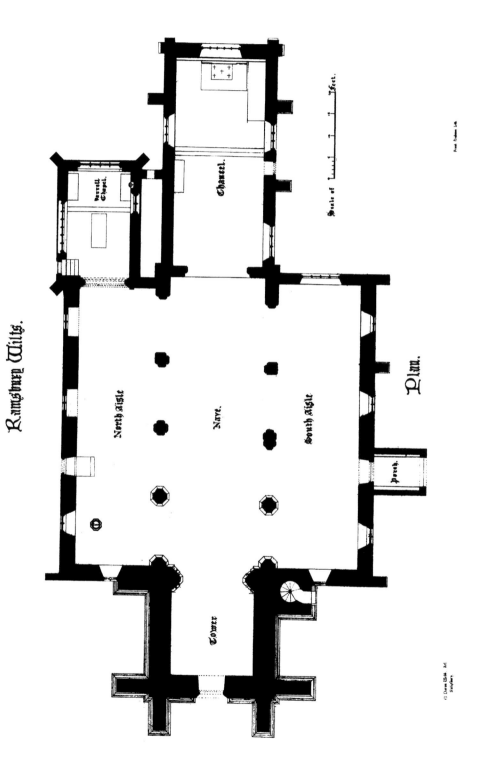

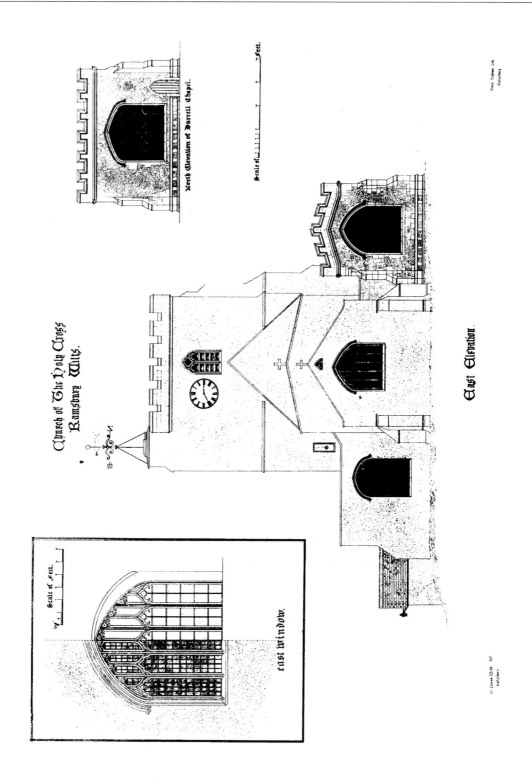

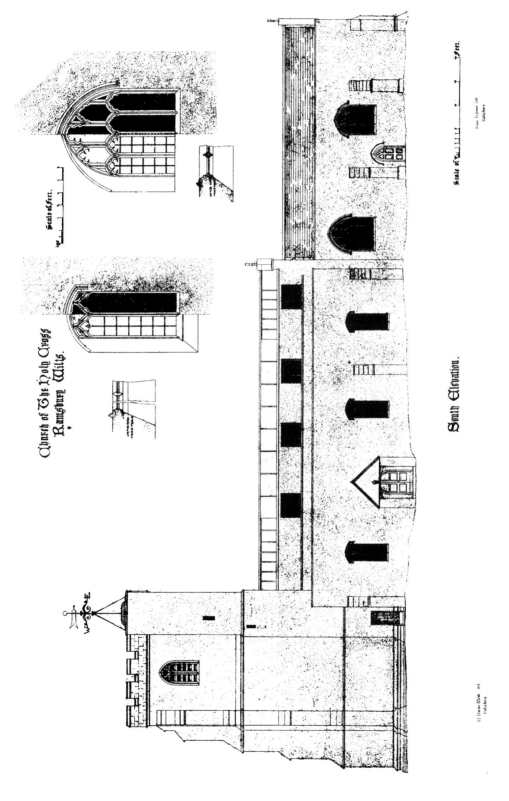

Church of The Holy Cross
Ramsbury Wilts.

South Elevation.

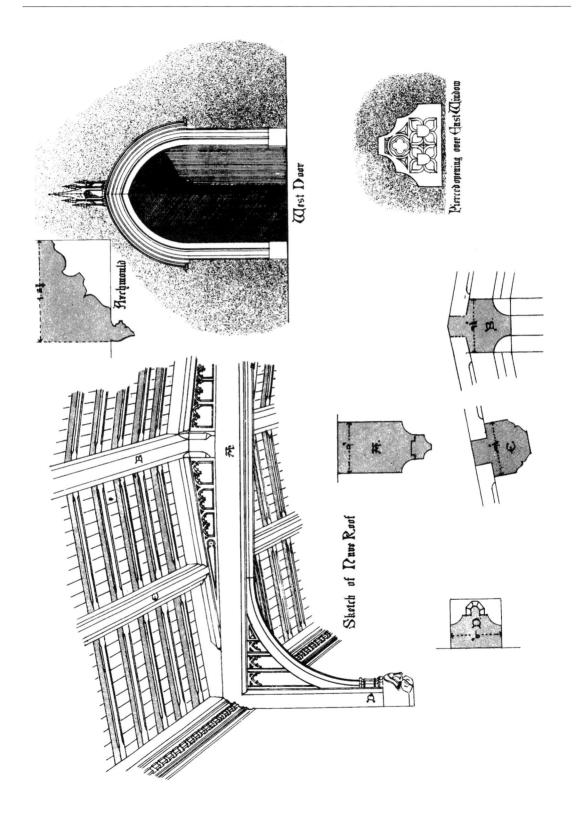

NOTES AND SUGGESTED READING

Notes

1 Rosemary Cramp, Emerita Professor of Archaeology (2004) 'Corpus of Anglo-Saxon Stone Sculpture', Dept. of Archaeology, University of Durham.

2 *Ibid.*

3 WRO, Holy Cross Church, Ramsbury, c.1710 seating plan.

4 WRO, Holy Cross Church, Ramsbury, c.1779 seating plan.

5 WRO 500 *passim*, Parish Registers.

6 Anderson, William (1990) *Green Man. The Archetype of our Oneness with the Earth,* Harper Collins: London.

7 Byard, Herbert (1967) 'Two old organs: Ramsbury and Lambourn', *The Organ*, No.184, Vol. xlvi, April 1967, p.173.

8 WRO, Bishops' Registers, Bishop Beauchamp, folio 150, 1453.

9 Sadler, A.G. *The Indents of the Lost Monumental Brasses of Wiltshire*; Kite, E. (1860) *The Monumental Brasses of Wiltshire.*

10 PRO, Cal. Pat. 1452-1461.

11 PRO, Cal.Pat. 1549.

12 WRO, Visitation Queries, 1864.

13 WRO, 500/26.

14 Batson, Revd A. Wellesley (c.1900) unpub.MS, 'A Retrospect of Half a Century'.

15 WAM xxii, p.235.

16 (Wiltshire) County Paper, Saturday August 12, 1893.

17 WRO, 500/27.

18 Webb, Edward Doran (1890) *The History of the Hundred of Ramsbury. Part 1. The Parish of Ramsbury,* Bennett Brothers: Salisbury, UK.

Quotations from the Bible are from the New Revised Standard Version (NRSV). Other quotations, with permission are from:

David Adam (1985) 'Circle me Lord' in *The Edge of Glory*, Triangle/SPCK: London.

John Betjeman (1958) 'From Church of England thoughts occasioned by hearing the bells of Magdalen Tower from the Botanic Garden, Oxford on St Mary Magdalen's Day' in *The Collected Poems*, 1975 ed., John Murray (Publishers) Ltd: London.

David J. Evans (1986) *Be Still*, Used by permission. *Adm. by worshiptogether.com songs excl. UK & Europe, adm. by kingswaymusic.tym@kingsway.co.uk.

George Herbert, 'Love' and 'Peace' in Wendy Cope (2002) *George Herbert. Verse and Prose*, SPCK: London.

Daniel Iverson (1935) *Spirit of the Living God*, 1963 ed., Birdwing Music/BMG Music Publishing: London.

Northumbrian Community (1994) *Celtic Night Prayer*, Marshall Pickering: London.

Suggested reading

MAJOR SOURCES:

Croucher, Barbara (1986) *The Village in the Valley. A History of Ramsbury*, Barbara Croucher: Ramsbury, UK.

Crowley, Douglas (1983) *Victoria County History of Wiltshire*, Vol.12, 'Ramsbury Hundred', Oxford University Press: Oxford.

OTHER SOURCES:

Bettey, J.H. (1987) *Church and parish. A Guide for Local Historians*, Batsford Local History Series, B.T.Batsford Ltd: London.

Blunt, Christopher, *A Guide to Ramsbury Parish Church.*
— (1959) unpub.MS, 'A Talk to the Wiltshire Archaeological Society'.

Davis, Courtney and O'Neill, Dennis (1999) *Celtic Beasts: Animal Motifs and Zoomorphic Design in Celtic Art*, Blandford.

De Paor, Maire (1979) *Early Irish Art*, Dept. of Foreign Affairs: Dublin.

Fletcher, Sir Bannister (1943) *A History of Architecture on the Comparative Method*, B.T.Batsford Ltd: London.

Gardner, A.H. (1949) *Outline of English Architecture*, B.T.Batsford Ltd: London.

Needham, A. (1944) *How to Study an Old Church*, 3rd ed. 1948, B.T.Batsford Ltd: London.

Parker, Admiral Hyde, *A Short History of Ramsbury Church.*

Pevsner, Sir Nikolaus (1963) *The Buildings of England. Wiltshire*, 2nd ed. revised, Bridget Cherry (1975), Yale University Press: New Haven and London.

Ramsbury Memoranda 1889-.

Rodwell, Warwick (1989) *English Heritage: Book of Church Archaeology*, B.T.Batsford Ltd/English Heritage: London.

Tatton-Brown, Tim (1989) *Great Cathedrals of Britain*, BBC Books: London.

Taylor, Richard (2003) *How to Read a Church*, Rider/Ebury Press: London.

Webb, Edward Doran (1890) *The History of the Hundred of Ramsbury. Part 1. The Parish of Ramsbury*, Bennett Brothers: Salisbury, UK.

West, Frank (1987) *St Michael's, Aldbourne*, St Michael's PCC.

INDEX

Page numbers in **bold** indicate special references. Page numbers in *italics* indicate illustrations.